A HANDBOOK FOR UNSTOPPABLE LEARNING

Laurie Robinson Sammons • Nanci N. Smith

Edited by Douglas Fisher and Nancy Frey

Solution Tree | Press

a division of Solution Tree

555 North Morton Street
Bloomington, IN 47404
800.733.6786 (toll free) / 812.336.7700
FAX: 812.336.7790

email: info@SolutionTree.com
SolutionTree.com

Visit **go.SolutionTree.com/instruction** to download the free reproducibles in this book.

Printed in the United States of America

21 20 19 18 17 1 2 3 4 5

Library of Congress Cataloging-in-Publication Data

Names: Sammons, Laurie Robinson, author. | Smith, Nanci N., author. | Fisher, Douglas, 1965- editor. | Frey, Nancy, 1959- editor.

Title: A handbook for unstoppable learning / authors, Laurie Robinson Sammons and Nanci N. Smith ; editors: Douglas Fisher and Nancy Frey.

Description: Bloomington, IN : Solution Tree Press, [2017] | Includes bibliographical references and index.

Identifiers: LCCN 2016055708 | ISBN 9781943874941 (perfect bound)

Subjects: LCSH: Effective teaching. | Teacher effectiveness. | Learning. | Teachers--Professional relationships.

Classification: LCC LB1025.3 .S2565 2017 | DDC 371.102--dc23 LC record available at https://lccn.loc.gov/2016055708

Solution Tree
Jeffrey C. Jones, CEO
Edmund M. Ackerman, President

Solution Tree Press
President and Publisher: Douglas M. Rife
Editorial Director: Sarah Payne-Mills
Managing Production Editor: Caroline Weiss
Senior Production Editor: Tara Perkins
Senior Editor: Amy Rubenstein
Copy Editor: Miranda Addonizio
Proofreader: Kendra Slayton
Text and Cover Designer: Laura Cox
Editorial Assistants: Jessi Finn and Kendra Slayton

Soli Deo Gloria

Acknowledgments

It has been stated over and over again that the highest form of flattery is imitation. Nothing could ring more true in education. As passionate advocates for active student engagement, we have learned alongside the very best mentors in the field: Richard DuFour and Becky DuFour, Jay McTighe, Grant Wiggins, Lucy Calkins, Carol Ann Tomlinson, Richard Allen, Douglas Fisher, Nancy Frey, Tim Kanold, Michael Fullan, David Sousa, and Robert Marzano, to name a few. We are fortunate to call many of these amazing educators our friends. We have watched their skillful preparation and delivery of strategies and protocols worth imitating. They model the model, so to speak, of sound and accurate instruction and leadership. And they are among many who we have followed and whose excellence and artfulness of teaching we have attempted to imitate through our own lens of innovation and student appropriateness.

We want to thank Claudia Wheatley for putting us together on this project and for her continued support and friendship.

We want to give special acknowledgment to our mentors, Douglas Fisher and Nancy Frey, who surround our work with the premises found in their book *Unstoppable Learning* (2015).

We could not do this work without the encouragement of our families! Thank you to our dear husbands, Frederick Sammons and Russ Smith, for their unwavering support and cheerleading into the wee hours of the morning and then again when the sun comes up. We thank our children, grandchildren, and extended families for their patience during this time of focused authorship. With hearts of deepest appreciation, we thank our treasured colleagues who work tirelessly, day after day, on behalf of children—our greatest natural resource.

Finally, we give our ultimate thanks to the Master Teacher, who has demonstrated that teaching is about serving with passion, extreme love, and humility.

Solution Tree Press would like to thank the following reviewers:

Joanne Keim
PBL Coordinator
Onondaga-Cortland-Madison BOCES
Syracuse, New York

Deborah A. Olson
Superintendent of Schools
Clinton Community School District
Clinton, Iowa

Genevie C. Rodríguez-Quiñones
Instructional Coach
Abydos/NJWP Writing Certified Trainer
Las Palmas Elementary School
San Antonio, Texas

Kris Schneider
Department Head, PLTW Engineering
Summit High School
Spring Hill, Tennessee

Randall Squier
Superintendent
Coxsackie-Athens Central School District
Coxsackie, New York

Steven Weber
Executive Director of Curriculum and Instruction
Chapel Hill-Carrboro City Schools
Chapel Hill, North Carolina

Visit **go.SolutionTree.com/instruction** to download the free reproducibles in this book.

Table of Contents

Reproducible pages are in italics.

We cannot, of course, save the world, because we do not have authority over its parts. We can serve the world though. This is everyone's calling, to lead a life that helps.

—Barry Lopez

About the Editors

Douglas Fisher, PhD, is professor of educational leadership at San Diego State University and a teacher leader at Health Sciences High and Middle College. He teaches courses in instructional improvement and formative assessment. As a classroom teacher, Fisher focuses on English language arts instruction. He was director of professional development for the City Heights Educational Collaborative and also taught English at Hoover High School.

Fisher received an International Reading Association Celebrate Literacy Award for his work on literacy leadership. For his work as codirector of the City Heights Professional Development Schools, Fisher received the Christa McAuliffe Award. He was corecipient of the Farmer Award for excellence in writing from the National Council of Teachers of English (NCTE) as well as the 2014 Exemplary Leader for the Conference on English Leadership, also from NCTE.

Fisher has written numerous articles on reading and literacy, differentiated instruction, and curriculum design. His books include *Teaching Students to Read Like Detectives*, *Checking for Understanding*, *Better Learning Through Structured Teaching*, and *Rigorous Reading*.

He earned a bachelor's degree in communication, a master's degree in public health, an executive master's degree in business, and a doctoral degree in multicultural education. Fisher completed postdoctoral study at the National Association of State Boards of Education focused on standards-based reforms.

Nancy Frey, PhD, is a professor of educational leadership at San Diego State University. She teaches courses on professional development, systems change, and instructional approaches for supporting students with diverse learning needs. Frey also teaches classes at Health Sciences High and Middle College in San Diego. She is a credentialed special educator, reading specialist, and administrator in California.

Before joining the university faculty, Frey was a public school teacher in Florida. She worked at the state level for the Florida Inclusion Network, helping districts design systems for supporting students with disabilities in general education classrooms.

She is the recipient of the 2008 Early Career Achievement Award from the Literacy Research Association and the Christa McAuliffe Award for excellence in teacher education from the American Association of State Colleges and Universities. She was corecipient of the Farmer Award for excellence in writing from the National Council of Teachers of English for the article "Using Graphic Novels, Anime, and the Internet in an Urban High School."

Frey is coauthor of *Text-Dependent Questions*, *Using Data to Focus Instructional Improvement*, and *Text Complexity*. She has written articles for *The Reading Teacher*, *Journal of Adolescent and Adult Literacy*, *English Journal*, *Voices in the Middle*, *Middle School Journal*, *Remedial and Special Education*, and *Educational Leadership*.

To book Douglas Fisher or Nancy Frey for professional development, contact pd@SolutionTree.com.

About the Authors

Laurie Robinson Sammons is an educational consultant who has used her curriculum expertise and passion for students to help schools develop sustainable professional learning communities (PLCs) in thirty-six U.S. states and eight countries. This includes fidelity to the standards, a consistent analysis of student work, explicit student feedback, quality interventions, and differentiated instruction.

In her forty-two years as an educator, Laurie has served as an outreach specialist and adjunct professor at the University of North Dakota, district curriculum coordinator of Grand Forks Public Schools, reading specialist, and student-centered practitioner. She is skilled in Kagan Cooperative Learning Strategies, Understanding by Design, Robert J. Marzano's instructional strategies, Pyramid Response to Intervention (PRTI), and differentiated instruction.

In 2002, Laurie received a Fulbright Teacher Scholarship in an exchange program focusing on educational reform in Japan. She has been a featured speaker at PRTI, PLC, and assessment conferences around the globe. As an active community member, she has served on many education foundations and nonprofit organizations dedicated to helping at-risk students in environments of poverty and academic failure.

Laurie received a bachelor's degree in education at Mayville State University in North Dakota and her master's in reading at the University of North Dakota, Grand Forks. Currently a resident of Estero, Florida, she is an activist in Christy's Cause, raising awareness and advocating prevention for child sex trafficking. Laurie plans to donate her profits from this book to this organization. Her greatest joys include her family, reading, traveling, and golfing.

Nanci N. Smith is currently a full-time national and international consultant and featured conference speaker in the areas of mathematics, curriculum and assessment, differentiated instruction, and mathematics professional learning communities. Her work includes professional development in forty-five U.S. states and nine countries. She has taught courses at the high school, undergraduate, and graduate levels.

Nanci is author of *A Mind for Mathematics: Meaningful Teaching and Learning in Elementary Classrooms* and *Every Math Learner: A Doable Approach to Teaching with Learning Differences in Mind, Grades K–5* and *Grades 6–12*. She is the consultant, designer, and author of the *Meaningful Math: Leading Students Toward Understanding and Application* DVD series and developed a National Science Foundation–funded CD and DVD professional development series for middle school mathematics teachers. She has published various chapters in the areas of differentiation, effective mathematics instruction, curriculum design, and standards implementation and has given interviews for online publications and National Public Radio. She has been a featured speaker for the National Council of Teachers of Mathematics national conference as well as numerous other conferences in the United States and abroad.

Nanci received her PhD in curriculum and instruction, mathematics education, from Arizona State University. She is a National Board–certified teacher in Adolescence and Young Adulthood/Mathematics. She lives in Phoenix, Arizona, with her husband Russ and three cats. Her passions are her family, especially her eight (soon to be nine) grandchildren, travel, and knitting. To learn more about Nanci's work, follow @DocNanci on Twitter.

To book Laurie Robinson Sammons or Nanci N. Smith for professional development, contact pd@SolutionTree.com.

Foreword

By Douglas Fisher and Nancy Frey

Teaching is more complex than most parents and politicians realize. It requires careful planning, strong relationships, and thoughtful interactions. Teachers have to design learning experiences that close the gap between what students currently know and can do and what they are supposed to be able to do. Following decades of research and teaching, we identified seven interrelated areas necessary for classrooms and schools to function effectively (Fisher & Frey, 2015). In our thinking, we divide the work of the teacher into these areas.

- Planning learning
- Launching learning
- Consolidating learning
- Assessing learning
- Adapting learning
- Managing learning
- Leading learning

In *Unstoppable Learning* (Fisher & Frey, 2015), we also note that these seven elements relate to, and in fact depend on, each other. For example, a change in classroom management procedures will impact students' collaborative learning time (consolidating), which can then alter the assessment evidence that students produce. Classrooms and schools are highly interdependent systems, and we realize now that professional learning efforts focused on one tiny aspect of teaching and learning, without attention to the other aspects, will not ensure growth for either the students or teachers.

For example, simply recommending that a teacher implement reciprocal teaching (which, according to published research, is highly effective) without talking about the changes required in planning, assessing, and managing learning is unfair and counterproductive. Further, efforts to squeeze reciprocal teaching (as an example) into an existing system, without making changes in the other elements, will likely result in teachers and administrators believing that reciprocal teaching does not work, at least for their students. When that happens, teachers and administrators often discard a perfectly good approach for helping students consolidate their learning and begin considering a new approach. That new approach is no more likely to work without changes to other parts of the system.

This handbook helps readers identify the ways in which systems thinking, and specifically the seven elements we describe in *Unstoppable Learning*, can be implemented in a cohesive way. Laurie Robinson Sammons and Nanci N. Smith provide readers with actionable items that they can use to unleash the power students have.

Sammons and Smith offer example after example that illustrate ways in which readers can apply the seven elements to support student learning. In addition, they note that collaborative planning teams, as part of professional learning communities (PLCs), can use the seven elements to strengthen their work. As teams discuss what students should learn, they can use the processes and approaches that Sammons and Smith recommend to build better units of study. Further, teams can identify which students have mastered the content and which need additional instruction or intervention as part of the assessing and adapting learning work that they do.

Having said that, we also appreciate the clear examples of high-quality instruction that Sammons and Smith provide. They profile effective teachers who launch students into learning and who make content relevant. They also provide recommendations for helping students consolidate their understanding. This is no easy feat, yet Sammons and Smith make it seem simple. In the grand scheme of things, it's fairly easy to tell students what to think and then have them relate that information back, whether that be orally, on a test, or in writing. It's significantly more complicated to design learning experiences that provide students an opportunity to really consolidate their understanding such that they own the skills, strategies, and content and can use their growing knowledge base to solve new problems, think creatively, and persevere when faced with adversity.

In sum, we hope that you find this handbook as useful as we did. It does a fine job of translating ideas into action that will enable more and more students to experience success in school. In doing so, more and more teachers will feel empowered, and their morale will improve. As educators, we have a lot to do, but our job boils down to helping students learn, whether that be about themselves and the world, new content, how to think strategically, or how to contribute to society. The ideas Sammons and Smith present in this handbook will allow educators to reach their goals, and students will learn more.

Introduction

We can probably all agree that education is one of the most important influences on our future. Education will impact our students' individual futures, society's future, the United States' future, and even the world's future. Our role as educators is incredibly important and, at the same time, incredibly challenging. Left unchecked, the demands from outside the classroom and expectations for learning inside the classroom can overpower the most important decisions teachers can make: the design for learning. However, we have more resources in education to prevent this—research, ideas, blogs, opinions, and so on—than ever before. In this book, we provide resources to try to make the complexities of effective classroom life understandable and manageable—focused and unstoppable.

Our Mission

The renowned Mayo Clinic in Rochester, Minnesota, which is known for the highest-quality patient care, has held to its century-old mission of "providing the best care to every patient through integrated clinical practice, education, and research" (Mayo Clinic, 2017). What power exists in this short but poignant message of hope! When parents of our valued next generation drop their children off at our classroom doors, how powerful it would be if each and every school could promise the same—the *best* care to *every* student through focused instruction and best-practice research. Certainly, we have worked alongside teachers in exemplary schools who have internalized these ideas and demonstrate consistent education practices worth replicating. Just imagine the dynamic results if we found that same mission living and breathing within every hall and every classroom of our schools across the globe.

In this book, we provide specific strategies and templates to support Douglas Fisher and Nancy Frey's (2015) Unstoppable Learning model and make this mission goal a reality in schools and classrooms. *Unstoppable Learning* describes seven elements essential for every classroom to tap into student potential: planning, launching, consolidating, assessing, adapting, managing, and leading (see figure I.1, page 2).

Systems Thinking and Professional Learning Communities

In order to ensure the excellent education that we all desire for every student, *systems thinking* needs to be a top priority. Douglas Fisher and Nancy Frey (2015) define systems thinking as "the ability to see the big picture, observe how the elements within a system influence one another, identify emerging patterns, and act on them in ways that fortify the structures within" (p. 2). Fisher and Frey (2015) look at the role of teachers as *systems managers* in order to maximize student learning, breaking the complexities of a classroom into understandable components that are viewed and managed as a system in order to increase students' unstoppable learning potential.

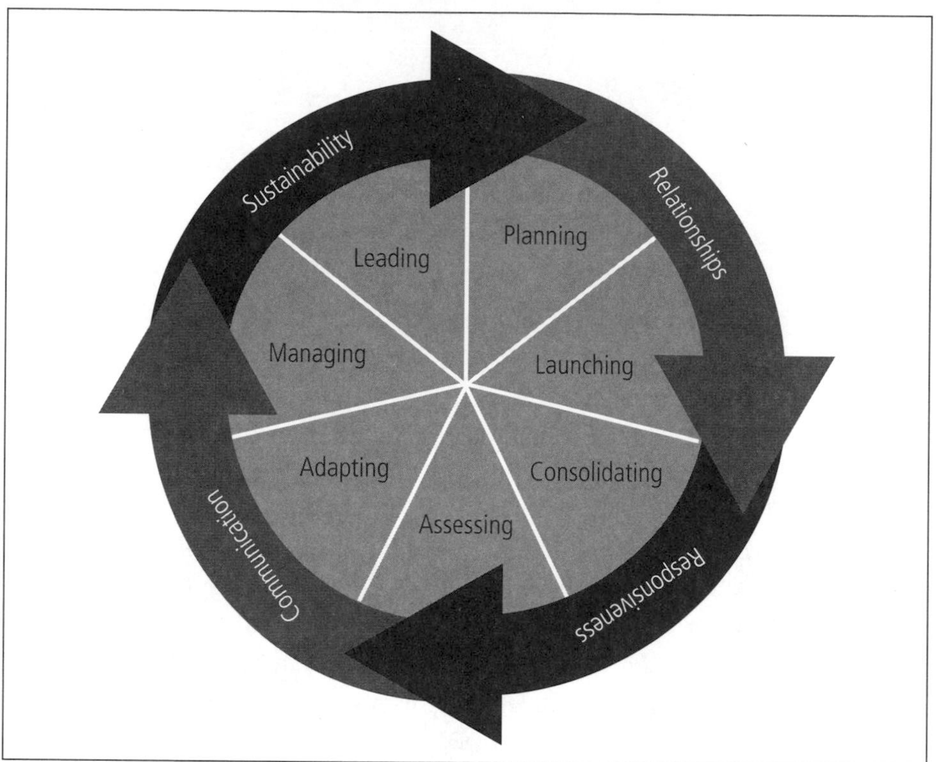

Source: Fisher & Frey, 2015.

Figure I.1: Components of Unstoppable Learning.

We apply systems thinking within our classrooms, but one of the most effective ways to broaden systems thinking is creating collaborative teams, which begins with the foundational professional learning community (PLC) work of Richard DuFour, Rebecca DuFour, Robert Eaker, Thomas Many, and Mike Mattos (2016). Throughout this book, we will use the term *systems team* to represent all staff within a school district from preK to grade 12. We acknowledge that even the power of one dedicated teacher can make a difference for students. However, from firsthand experience establishing collaborative team discussions with one mission, one vision, and one huge commitment to systemwide student learning, we state with confidence that when preK–12 teachers work in tandem with the same intended goal, increased student proficiency is likely to occur faster and with heightened accountability and sustainability. Designing effective instruction for Unstoppable Learning begins with fierce and crucial conversations at every grade level and in every content area. These conversations focus on the four critical questions of a PLC (DuFour et al., 2016) and one additional question for our work.

1. What do students need to know and be able to do?
2. How will we know that students have learned?
3. What will we do when students have not learned?
4. When students already know the content, what do we do?

The answers to these questions reside within our fifth critical question.

5. What instructional practices must we embed to ensure that students learn?

We address these questions throughout the chapters of this book, as we have found that these five critical questions and systems thinking in the classroom are entwined. For those who work in a PLC, considering these questions within the context of Unstoppable Learning will deepen and significantly connect to classroom practice. For those who do not, the five critical questions can serve as guiding reflections to consider. We wholeheartedly contend that when job-alike or grade-level teams plan common lessons and assessments, there is no place to go but up where learning is concerned.

Chapter Overviews

The chapters of this book each align with one of the seven areas Fisher and Frey (2015) establish as necessary for Unstoppable Learning (with chapter 6 addressing the areas of both managing and leading). Chapter 1 focuses on planning a curriculum based on the most essential content students need to know, understand, and be able to do. We introduce the acronym CUES as the foundation for curriculum planning to help teachers *choose*, *unpack*, and *engage students* in the standards. These components become the foundation for specific lesson plans and eventual assessments. Using this structure enables us to avoid the wide but shallow coverage model and instead dive deep into the content.

Chapter 2 explores the most effective ways we can create good beginnings and launch a lesson or unit to ensure that students are engaged and invested in the learning. We examine the importance of writing focused learning targets to ensure that the learning objectives are clear to students. We draw on cognitive science to inform us as to how lessons should optimally begin in order to facilitate greater understanding and long-term memory storage. This includes ensuring that students know what they will be learning in the upcoming lesson using strategies to excite and invite students into learning.

Chapter 3 further addresses how we can make the learning relevant for students and focuses on how to define rigor as well as selecting and implementing rigorous tasks. We discuss what true student engagement looks like, with many examples and descriptions of engaging tasks and strategies to offer students that will help them consolidate their learning.

Chapter 4 provides guidance on assessing student learning to ensure accurate understanding of what students have learned. We note how to gather evidence and make it the basis for our assessments. We examine each type of assessment: preassessment, formative assessment, checks for understanding, summative assessment, and student self-assessment.

Chapter 5 addresses how adapting instruction by differentiating for students' unique needs and learning styles can produce improved learning outcomes for students who have not learned the content or who already know the content. This chapter addresses the reality of the student differences we encounter daily in our classrooms. We explain the common sense of differentiation with multiple strategies and examples. Of course, all of this takes place in the classroom where teachers *manage* and *lead* learning.

Chapter 6 discusses the fine-tuning involved in being the head coach in the classroom. We address how to establish and maintain a healthy learning environment and what to do when there are inevitable off-task behaviors. We also offer guidance on ways faculty and administrators alike can assume leadership and management roles to strengthen collaborative work in schools and across the district, whether with singleton teachers or collaborative teams.

These chapters contain many lesson examples to help readers implement the ideas in this book and in *Unstoppable Learning*. We provide numerous templates to take educators step by step through the process of purposeful design. We have interspersed what we call Ponder Boxes, indicated with the symbol to the left, throughout the book and placed reflection questions at the end of each chapter to encourage readers to think deeply about the content and form their own conclusions and next steps. An appendix offers tools to help put all the pieces of the Unstoppable Learning model together in practice.

Background on Featured Strategies

While the elements of Unstoppable Learning are a system and thus interdependent, after gaining the foundational information in chapter 1, readers can use the chapters in this book in any order. We believe that the first chapter, planning, should be the first step in any curriculum or instructional design, and many of the elements we discuss and templates we provide in this chapter are foundational to the other chapters. From there, readers should feel free to jump to any chapter they want.

Though some of the strategies in this book are not new, they have gone through several iterations to meet current educational standards for college and career readiness. Reaching back to the late 1970s to the early 1990s, early in our careers as educators, we used many of these basic tools with a different twist. The disappointing truth is that throngs of teachers from around the globe have abandoned many of their student-successful strategies due to all the heavy demands of various government mandates. We want to encourage teachers that the only way to help our students achieve is through excellent instruction, including the strategies we know work. We certainly have enough evidence at this point through both research and personal experiences to prove that merely covering topics just doesn't stick with students.

We believe in the underpinnings of established standards to promote excellence. Whether teachers are using the Common Core State Standards (CCSS) or their own state's rigorous standards, in the context of our book, it makes no difference. We applaud and honor all the hard-working educators who give their time, talents, and love to nurture our next generation, despite the heavy demands. Instructional design is a thoughtful, whole-to-part process focused on genuine, meaningful, and authentic lifelong learning. Embracing that monumental task, we, too, are invested in assisting and supporting our valued teacher colleagues, who work tirelessly day after day to make a difference in the lives of students.

How teachers plan for and use instructional or assessment tools can either enrich or defeat a student's experience. We must know the specific function it serves to determine how to use it most effectively. With that in mind, we have reached deep into our treasure trove of classroom goodies and selected tools that we know from firsthand experience work for students and teachers. Relevancy is our key, and we are confident we can add new tools to any reader's as we have done for many teachers in training sessions who have approached us to tell us directly how valuable these tools and ideas have been to them. As practitioners, we hope that this book will stir up and rejuvenate new thoughts and innovation.

Finally, we encourage readers to do as we have done and *revise*, *transform*, and *innovate* this information according to the diverse population of students they serve. Read, reflect, and enjoy!

CHAPTER 1

PLANNING FOCUSED AND PURPOSEFUL CURRICULUM

What comes to mind when you think of planning? How much time do you invest in the deep and thoughtful understanding and planning of the content to be taught? We confess—when we both began teaching, we thought planning meant going through the textbook, practicing the examples, and possibly finding an additional way to practice before starting homework. We would start class by reviewing homework. Next would come direct instruction, introducing the new material. Then we would practice the new material. Here we could be creative and find puzzle-type worksheets or occasionally design a new game or activity to keep our students engaged. Finally, if there was time after lecture and large-group practice, students could begin their homework in the last few minutes of the class period.

At that time, planning was about the prep work. Truthfully, we vividly remember being handed a beautifully tabbed, hundred-pound binder containing the state standards. We stashed the binder on a shelf and then rarely ever opened it. We knew what we were supposed to teach (the text, pages 1–400) and made certain not to skip any of the major concepts during the year.

We have come a long way since then. We now rely heavily on meaningful and deep discussions centered around state standards, and then we design instruction accordingly. When we consider planning, we know the process is multifaceted, complex, and much richer when we engage in understanding the standards in a collegial huddle rather than as an individual silo as in days gone by. However, whether you are fortunate enough to work collaboratively, or you work predominantly as a singleton teacher, the time spent planning is the foundation for success.

In some ways, this entire book is about planning—thoughtful, systematic planning with the end in mind. Every chapter covers topics that teachers must plan before bringing to the classroom. For example, we can't launch a lesson if we haven't deliberately planned how to launch the lesson. We can't give a meaningful assessment that we have not thoughtfully planned and aligned to the standards from which we deliberately instruct.

If practitioners do not spend the time to dig deeply into the standards from which they base the unit, they will not know if the instruction they deliver affords their students the opportunity to learn the expected content at the required depth. We intend for this chapter to help teachers focus and lay the foundation in order to intentionally plan all the other components. They can do so by addressing the need for deeper learning through a focused curriculum based on prioritized standards. In this chapter, we will examine the need for deeper learning and look at ways to clarify instruction through planning, prioritize standards, and analyze standards. We will also discuss how singletons can approach these items.

Understanding the Need for Deeper Learning

According to Programme for International Student Assessment (PISA) reports (Organisation for Economic Co-operation and Development [OECD], n.d.; OECD, 2016), the United States has fallen behind its international counterparts in the education world. But statistics alone don't tell the whole, rich education story of the United States. While many nations take a more concentrated and rigorous stance on teaching fewer standards with depth and understanding, the United States teaches more content in less depth (Marzano, 2001). For example, a typical eighth-grade mathematics textbook in Japan usually has ten major topics while one in the United States has thirty-two (Schmidt, Houang, & Cogan, 2002). We refer to the U.S. approach as *curriculum snorkeling* because it covers many topics in less depth, just as a snorkeler can cover a large area but must stay near the surface of the water, unable to uncover what lies deeper. Conversely, a *deep-sea diving* approach takes time to teach fewer concepts well and with intensity to intentionally explore deep, rich content with rich discussion to reach profound understanding. In a nutshell, we have been masters of providing a well-rounded mile-wide curriculum about many things but have only gone an inch deep in their understanding and application. That philosophy comes with assets and liabilities. Our students are exposed to a greater assortment of topics but do not develop the depth of understanding or problem-solving skills that students in other countries do.

With the adoption of the Common Core State Standards (CCSS) and other state standards that are equally focused, we have seized the opportunity to exchange the snorkeling mentality for a deep-sea diving approach. This means we value fewer, deeper, and more sophisticated standards and implement them with *fidelity*, which promises dependability, consistency, and reliability, with those implementing the curriculum all on the same page about what will be taught. In essence, the CCSS and similar state standards are fewer in number, more concentrated, and designed with greater rigor and real-world application. The United States is repurposing and repositioning its course for fewer standards done well and deep. But this will take time and patience as the political and parental public raises questions about the intensity and reliability of the standards' requirements.

The good news is that in systems thinking, preK–12 teams and teachers who learn to prioritize the standards and gain clarity about the content provide the foundation on which all other components of the system depend—the investment is worth every minute of time it requires. Whether immersing oneself in conversations regarding standards or embracing one's own district or state curriculum documents, clarifying what students must learn is critical. Teachers who do not run the risk of ending up teaching what they think is best or like the most. This approach results in curricular chaos and designed units that do not meet the intended curriculum as defined by the standards. Not only do students need to know the standards—they also need to apply the standards. We must teach for what students need to *know*, *understand*, and *do*. Throughout the book, we use the acronym *KUD* to refer to this concept.

Certainly, there are some advantages to offering multiple electives and a broad experience base in school; however, these unfortunately come at the expense of necessary time in essential classes to develop the conceptual understandings, connections, and 21st century skills that our high school graduates need. While the surface-snorkeling effect gives curricular variety, it fails to produce the skills students need to dive into the content and be articulators of deep knowledge. See the reproducible "Questions for Expectations and Rigor" (page 19) for team discussion or individual reflection questions to consider regarding the larger picture of expectations and rigor.

Clarifying Instruction Through Planning

In the reality TV show *The Amazing Race* (van Munster & Weinsein, 2001), teams try to solve clues that lead them to a specific location, and if they are correct, they find the next clue at that location. This continues until the teams finish at a specific location. The first teams to reach the final location stay on the show for the next episode, and the last team is eliminated. Unfortunately, some teams misread the clues and end up in the wrong place. We have seen this happen with hard-working teachers as well, who sometimes do not understand the depth or complexity required by standards, read a standard in isolation instead of considering the grouping of standards for the entire unit to develop the bigger picture, or do not choose a strong instructional or assessment approach aligned to the standards.

To avoid misreading the intention of the standards, we must begin clarifying instruction by focusing on a unit before focusing on specific lessons. One of the greatest challenges in planning focused and purposeful curriculum is postponing our natural tendency as teachers to jump to specific lessons or activities. How often do teachers read a standard and think, "I have a great activity for this!"? It is important to look at all of the standards on which a unit of study is built to analyze and prioritize them before thinking of the more specific daily lesson or activity. As noted in the introduction, we must intentionally *choose* the standards, *unpack* the standards, and plan to *engage students* with the standards. Throughout the book, we use the acronym CUES to refer to this concept. Planning the whole before the parts in this way enables the parts to come together. For this reason, we have designed a unit-planning template (figure 1.1, pages 8–9) to use while planning a unit. We provide the complete blank template here for reference. However, in each chapter, we will isolate different aspects of the template and illustrate gradually throughout the book how to complete the template. Note that the items on the bottom half of the template are provided for users' own recording and planning purposes. Because these are rather self-explanatory, we do not discuss their generation and development in depth. Visit **go.SolutionTree.com/instruction** to access free reproducible sample units that illustrate these portions.

Without considering all of the standards together and *then* designing lessons, it is possible to end up at the wrong location. Even worse, this would mean our students also end up in the wrong location. Our goal in unit design is to be able to execute standards well and deeply, thus creating a guaranteed and viable curriculum (Marzano, 2003). If you teach in a district that has not yet engaged in the process of creating a guaranteed and viable curriculum, in addition to chapters 1 and 2 of this book, see the blog post "How Guaranteed and Viable Is Your Curriculum?" (Ferriter, 2012) to build background information and access user-friendly handouts.

When teachers are confident their unit design is complete and has established a guaranteed and viable curriculum, they move on to the specific lesson design. Figure 1.2 (page 10) offers a template readers can use as a guide as they design their lessons within a unit. As with the unit-planning template, we provide the complete blank template here for reference, but the following chapters will detail specific portions of the template, piece by piece.

A guaranteed curriculum requires teachers to provide *all* students with a robust curriculum surrounded with similar opportunities to grow regardless of who they are or their demographic profile. A viable curriculum must be doable within the nine months we have to teach students each year. We can accomplish this through prioritizing and analyzing standards.

Unit Title: ____________ **Subject Area:** ____________ **Grade Level:** ______

Identified Standards and Benchmarks (CUES):

Suggested Time Frame (Grading Period)

☐ Q1 ☐ Q2 ☐ Q3 ☐ Q4

Priority Standards

☐ ____________
☐ ____________
☐ ____________
☐ ____________
☐ ____________
☐ ____________
☐ ____________
☐ ____________
☐ ____________
☐ ____________
☐ ____________
☐ ____________
☐ ____________

Unit Topic and Universal Theme

Describe what this unit is about. What are the big ideas and skills that students will develop in the unit?

Understandings

List the essential understandings for your unit. Students will understand that . . .

Essential Questions

Applications (Do)

List the Do for your unit, including possible applications.

Know

List Knows for your unit, including essential vocabulary.

☐ ____________
☐ ____________
☐ ____________
☐ ____________
☐ ____________
☐ ____________
☐ ____________
☐ ____________
☐ ____________
☐ ____________
☐ ____________

Formative and Summative Assessments

☐ ____________
☐ ____________
☐ ____________
☐ ____________
☐ ____________
☐ ____________
☐ ____________
☐ ____________
☐ ____________
☐ ____________

Bloom's Taxonomy Integration

Creating: ____________

Evaluating: ____________

Analyzing: ____________

Applying: ____________

Understanding: ____________

Remembering: ____________

Technology Integration

- ☐ ____________
- ☐ ____________
- ☐ ____________
- ☐ ____________
- ☐ ____________
- ☐ ____________
- ☐ ____________
- ☐ ____________
- ☐ ____________
- ☐ ____________
- ☐ ____________
- ☐ ____________
- ☐ ____________

Prior Knowledge Needed

Common Student Misconceptions in the Unit

Differentiation and Interventions

Reflection

Resources and Materials

- ☐ ____________
- ☐ ____________
- ☐ ____________
- ☐ ____________
- ☐ ____________
- ☐ ____________
- ☐ ____________
- ☐ ____________
- ☐ ____________
- ☐ ____________
- ☐ ____________
- ☐ ____________
- ☐ ____________
- ☐ ____________
- ☐ ____________
- ☐ ____________
- ☐ ____________
- ☐ ____________

Example Activities and Instructional Strategies

- ☐ ____________
- ☐ ____________
- ☐ ____________
- ☐ ____________
- ☐ ____________
- ☐ ____________
- ☐ ____________
- ☐ ____________
- ☐ ____________
- ☐ ____________
- ☐ ____________
- ☐ ____________
- ☐ ____________
- ☐ ____________
- ☐ ____________

Figure 1.1: Unit-planning template.

Visit ***go.SolutionTree.com/instruction*** *for a free reproducible version of this figure.*

KUD for Lesson (From Unit Plan): **Know:** **Understand:** **Do:**		
Learning Target:		
Activity	**Class Structure**	**Time**
Launch Activity	_______ Whole class _______ Small group _______ Pairs _______ Individual	
Engagement Activity 1 Differentiation:	_______ Whole class _______ Small group _______ Pairs _______ Individual	
Engagement Activity 2 Differentiation:	_______ Whole class _______ Small group _______ Pairs _______ Individual	
Engagement Activity 3 Differentiation:	_______ Whole class _______ Small group _______ Pairs _______ Individual	
Engagement Activity 4 Differentiation:	_______ Whole class _______ Small group _______ Pairs _______ Individual	
Engagement Activity 5 Differentiation:	_______ Whole class _______ Small group _______ Pairs _______ Individual	
Formative Assessment and Check for Understanding:	_______ Whole class _______ Small group _______ Pairs _______ Individual	
Closure Activity:	_______ Whole class _______ Small group _______ Pairs _______ Individual	

Figure 1.2: Lesson-plan template.

Visit ***go.SolutionTree.com/instruction*** *for a free reproducible version of this figure.*

Prioritizing Standards

Often, there are still too many standards, and many are confusing and poorly constructed. This is another example of the *curriculum snorkeling* concept in action. Too often, teachers work tirelessly to structure a multitude of meaningful lessons to prepare students for high-stakes tests, yet students do not reach deep understanding of the standards, and there is still not enough time to cover all the content and reteach the areas needing additional attention.

Kelly Gallagher (2009), a teacher at Magnolia High School in Anaheim, California, and former codirector of the South Basin Writing Project, states, "When teachers try to cram twenty-two years of curriculum into a K–12 time frame, everyone loses. Students develop into memorizers instead of into thinkers" (p. 11). Prioritizing standards will address the time crunch that too much content and too little time create.

We must acknowledge that some standards demand more time for students to learn them well than others. We caution teachers not to confuse the process of teams (preferably) or individual teachers prioritizing standards with eliminating any of them. It is simply developing a hierarchy of essential learning targets surrounded and supported by the less weighted ones. All of them are important, but essential learning targets are the targets we gain when we go deep-sea diving—they go deeply and provide strength and stability. Our less-weighted targets, those we might encounter when snorkeling, fill gaps to support our essential targets.

How do we determine which standards require SCUBA gear and which need a snorkel? According to Larry Ainsworth (2010), a *priority standard* is one that provides students the prerequisite knowledge and skills needed to know and understand grade-level content. While we use the term *priority standard*, you may have also heard these referred to as *power standards* and *essential standards*. For our purposes, we consider these terms to be synonymous with one another. Another reference worth sharing is the term *promise standards* used in relation to priority standards. We love the idea of these most important standards being a promise to reach and teach our students these important concepts, and that all students receive equal access to this essential learning.

A *supporting standard* is one that enables a student to perform the priority standard successfully and acts as a preliminary stepping stone or scaffold. Selecting priority standards allows for complete clarity and consistency in teaching the intended curriculum. It also allows a hybrid opportunity for necessary skill development essential for lifetime learning *and* in school test-taking situations. But one does not exclude the other. We invite those who have not yet taken the opportunity to focus the curricular lens (or their schools or districts) to use the following protocol for prioritizing standards to not only save precious instructional time but also ensure a guaranteed and viable experience done well and deeply.

When teams establish fidelity to the priority standards, they filter their discussions around five criteria. Three of the criteria (endurance, readiness, and leverage) originate from Ainsworth (2010), and for the purpose of addressing the reality of today's classroom demands, we have added two additional criteria (teacher input and testing mandates).

1. **Endurance:** Will the knowledge and skills of this standard endure long after this lesson, into the next grade, and beyond these classroom walls into life application?
2. **Readiness:** Will the knowledge and skills of this standard prepare students to be successful in the next grade level or course?
3. **Leverage:** Will the knowledge and skills of this standard be of value in other content areas?
4. **Teacher input:** Is it necessary for my students to know and understand this standard before leaving my classroom at the end of this year?
5. **Testing mandates:** Will students need the knowledge and skills of this standard to perform proficiently on important classroom, district, state, or national tests?

Figure 1.3 provides a template to begin the process of prioritizing standards. Single classroom teachers, vertical grade bands (K–2, 3–5, 6–8, 9–12), or grade-level or content-area teams can all use this tool. The process is exactly the same for each group. By far the greatest benefit from the process is the deep and rich conversation teachers engage in regarding content and instructional fidelity.

Place an X in the column that meets the criteria of a priority standard.						
Standard	**Teacher Input**	**Endurance**	**Readiness**	**Leverage**	**Testing Mandates**	**Priority Standard? (Yes or No)**
1. Students will write persuasively.						
2. Students will be able to identify parts of speech (noun, verb, adverb, preposition, and so on).						
3. Students will persevere in problem solving.						

Figure 1.3: Prioritizing standards template.

*Visit **go.SolutionTree.com/instruction** for a free reproducible version of this figure.*

When teachers have marked four or five categories, they have established a priority standard. When they have checked two or three categories, they have determined a supporting standard. There are times when some teachers on the same team will check three categories and another teacher checks four categories for the very same standard. Group consensus is critical. The clarifying conversations that emerge from these differences will lead to an informed, final decision based on consensus. However, we advise that individual teachers first score their standards alone and then make the final selections when they come together as a collaborative team. When teachers have determined the priority standards, they should enter them in the Priority Standards column on the left-hand side of the unit-planning template (see figure 1.1, pages 8–9). Figure 1.4 shows an example of how one team listed its priority standards.

Priority Standards

- ☐ *Represent fractions with various models*
- ☐ *Interpret fractions as division*
- ☐ *Add and subtract fractions with like and unlike denominators*
- ☐ *Multiply fractions and a whole number by a fraction*
- ☐ *Divide a whole number by a unit fraction and a unit fraction by a whole number*
- ☐ *Solve real-world problems involving fractions and all operations*

Figure 1.4: Example of priority standards in a unit-planning template.

A common sentiment we hear from teachers is, "Why can't the district determine which standards are a priority? It would save us so much time and allow us to just teach!" We believe that teachers will not feel invested or informed in the process until they personally evaluate and determine what deserves their greatest instructional attention. More than the product they create, it is the investment of time, conversation, and negotiation that clarifies the essential student expectations toward proficiency. The learning gained when students deeply understand the content enriches everything that happens in the classroom as well.

Analyzing Standards

Once teachers have established what they need to teach with greatest priority, the next step is to analyze the standards on which to base the unit. This requires the process of unpacking the standards into what students should *know*, *understand*, and be able to *do* by the end of the unit. This work will ensure the lessons teachers design reach the required rigor and develop the conceptual understanding the standard requires. It will also determine the appropriate level of rigor to expect in the standard. So what do the terms *know*, *understand*, and *do* really mean?

When we talk about the *know* of a standard, we mean the factual content. Students can memorize the know—they can even google it. We often forget much of what we come to know in school. For example, many adults probably don't remember all of the state capitals of the United States. Truthfully, this does not bother us too much because we can find the capital of any state in seconds using our smartphones. Knowledge is important, and we can't go far in our learning without the basic knowledge that makes up the content. However, if we only teach for knowing, we are definitely limiting our sea exploration to snorkeling close to the surface. Students who only know are likely to be unable to transfer their learning into new situations, because to do so requires understanding (Wiggins & McTighe, 2011).

Understanding provides the depth of learning and refers to concepts, not facts. Understanding connects topics and subjects and supplies the answers to questions like, "Why do I have to learn this?" It connects multiple topics horizontally (across units throughout the school year) but also vertically (year after year). In fact, if it appears a student has gained understanding in just one lesson, it is undoubtedly *not* actually an understanding. For example, a student can *know* the definition of an adjective, but he or she needs to *understand* that adjectives add the color and feeling that make writing come alive to a reader. Students revisit this understanding over time and with various authors. It lends credence to the author's voice, and it matures the more the student writes and incorporates strategic word choice. In the same way, a student can *know* addition mathematics facts, but he or she needs to *understand* that only things that are alike can be added because addition and subtraction are operations that give a final count of things that are alike. In history, students need to *know* the specific causes, players, dates, and battles of World War I, but they need to *understand* that an imbalance between personal rights and outside power can lead to conflict. In biology, students come to *know* the parts of a plant, but they need to *understand* that living things are made up of interdependent parts, and when one part is injured or fails, the entire living entity is hurt. Understanding is where the deep-sea diving of learning occurs.

Finally, the *do* is what students will be able to do as a result of both knowing and understanding. When we write the *do* from the standards, we are not writing specific activities; we are looking for evidence of both knowing and understanding. For example, a student will be able to identify adjectives in a piece of writing and explain the impact of the author's word choice on the reader, or a student will write using appropriate adjectives in order to make writing come to life.

Ponder Box

Think of your favorite content area. How would you explain the difference between students who know your content, understand your content, and can do your content? How do you recognize students who understand versus students who know? What is the difference in what students are able to do when they know versus when they know and understand?

Figure 1.5 (page 14) gives examples of KUDs for each of the core-content areas (English language arts [ELA], mathematics, social studies, and science) based on sample standards. Visit **go.SolutionTree.com/instruction** for a blank template to use for writing KUDs for a unit.

<table>
<tr><td colspan="3">ELA standard: Describe characters in a story (e.g., their traits, motivations, or feelings) and explain how their actions contribute to the sequence of events (RL.3.3; National Governors Association Center for Best Practices & Council of Chief State School Officers [NGA & CCSSO], 2010a).</td></tr>
<tr><th>Know</th><th>Understand</th><th>Do</th></tr>
<tr><td>Elements of stories
How to find details
Plot sequence
Supporting evidence</td><td>Details and examples from texts help explain what the text is really saying to us.
Authors use details that may seem unimportant to create vivid characters, paint vivid settings, and advance the plot.</td><td>Choose a character and describe what the character looks like and thinks about. Offer evidence from the text.
Explain how your character relates to other characters, and use evidence from the text to support your explanation.
Demonstrate how your character interacts with and advances the plot of your story.</td></tr>
<tr><td colspan="3">Mathematics standard: Compute unit rates associated with ratios of fractions, including ratios of lengths, areas, and other quantities measured in like or different units (7.RPA.1; NGA & CCSSO, 2010b).</td></tr>
<tr><th>Know</th><th>Understand</th><th>Do</th></tr>
<tr><td>Vocabulary: rate, unit rate, proportion
How to represent proportional relationships in various forms
How to find a unit rate</td><td>Proportions describe real world relationships and allow us to make comparisons.
A unit rate determines a base rate from which comparisons and predictions are made.
Ratios and rates are comparisons of parts to parts, parts to wholes, or wholes to parts.</td><td>Determine unit rates and make comparisons and predictions in the real world (for example, best buys, package deals, mileage, and so on).
Explain the differences among a rate, unit rate, and fraction.
Represent and solve proportional relationships in various forms and contexts.</td></tr>
<tr><td colspan="3">Social studies standard: Compare the point of view of two or more authors for how they treat the same or similar topics, including which details they include and emphasize in their respective accounts (RH.9-10.6; NGA & CCSSO, 2010a).</td></tr>
<tr><th>Know</th><th>Understand</th><th>Do</th></tr>
<tr><td>Vocabulary: perspective, inference, fact, opinion
Details on specific topic
Authors' backgrounds</td><td>Different authors' perspectives on an event will determine each author's truth about the event.</td><td>Compare and contrast opposing views of a topic or event with supporting detail.
Explain the role of perspective in shaping truth.
Choose a side of a controversial topic and defend it using evidence. Refute the evidence of the other side.</td></tr>
<tr><td colspan="3">Science standard: Develop models to describe that organisms have unique and diverse life cycles but all have in common birth, growth, reproduction, and death (3-LS1-1; NGSS Lead States, 2013).</td></tr>
<tr><th>Know</th><th>Understand</th><th>Do</th></tr>
<tr><td>Vocabulary: life cycle, stages
Specific life stages for organisms being analyzed
Specific types of models</td><td>All living things go through similar stages of a life cycle, although specific details at each stage differ.
Different models can explain and exhibit life cycles in different ways, and each model can show differing aspects in different ways.</td><td>Depict similarities and differences in life cycles among different organisms.
Model different organisms' life cycles.</td></tr>
</table>

Figure 1.5: Example KUDs for an instructional unit.

Visit ***go.SolutionTree.com/instruction*** *for a free reproducible version of this figure.*

The examples in figure 1.5 use single standards to show how KUDs are developed. Teachers should consider each standard. However, each standard will not necessarily be unpacked individually. This is because the standards within a unit will overlap and complement each other. Regard the standards collectively, and develop KUDs for the whole unit. There are no hard and fast rules, other than that knowing has to do with facts and understanding with concepts. Steps or how-tos are always placed in the Know column.

The Understand column is usually the most challenging to write. Generally, there are only two to five understandings in a unit. Teachers should write them as complete sentences and preface them with the phrase, *Students will understand that . . . .* The word *that* is essential to writing understandings because it will help complete the thought, and there will be a greater likelihood that the sentence written will be conceptual rather than factual. Do not use *how* in its place or just use *Students will understand . . . .* For example, *Students will understand how World War I started* is not an understanding. The list of causes of World War I are factual and would be listed under the Know column. Instead, *Students will understand that multiple facets come together to cause conflict and wars* is a more global, conceptual understanding. Other ideas could relate to power and struggle or other lenses through which teachers want their students to consider the causes of war. *Students will understand the use of adjectives* is also not an understanding. One *knows* how to use adjectives. However, *Students will understand that word choice impacts a reader's understanding and visualization of a text* is a more global, conceptual understanding about adjectives (as well as other parts of speech) than merely knowing how to use an adjective.

Know List Knows for your unit, including essential vocabulary.
☐ *Review vocabulary terms: fraction, numerator, deonominator, whole, part, mixed number, equivalent fraction, common multiple, least common multiple, denominator* ☐ *New vocabulary terms: unit fraction, benchmark fractions, improper fractions* ☐ *How to model fractions concretely and visually* ☐ *Numerators always represent the number of parts of a whole that are selected, and denominators represent the number of total parts in the whole* ☐ *Methods for finding common denominators* ☐ *Estimation techniques, especially with benchmark fractions* ☐ *Fractions are another way to represent division* ☐ *How to convert between mixed numbers and improper fractions* ☐ *Strategies to add, subtract, multiply, and divide with fractions and mixed numbers*

Figure 1.6: Example of Knows in a unit-planning template.

Once teachers have determined the KUDs for their units, they should enter them in the unit-planning template under the Know column on the right-hand side, and the Understandings and Applications (Do) boxes in the center (see figure 1.1, pages 8–9). See figures 1.6, 1.7 (page 16), and figure 1.8 (page 16) for examples of how one team listed its Knows, Understandings, and Dos in their unit-planning template for a fifth-grade unit on fraction operations. Visit **go.SolutionTree.com/instruction** to view a complete sample unit plan for fraction operations, as well as an additional complete example of a sixth-grade unit plan on the Renaissance.

The KUDs for each unit become the basis for every lesson and every assessment within the unit. In fact, the lesson-plan template we introduced in figure 1.2 (page 10) begins with writing the specific KUD from the unit plan to address in the lesson. Figure 1.9 (page 17) provides an example of a KUD that a teacher would enter in the lesson-plan template for the specific lesson.

Understanding

List the essential Understandings for your unit. Students will understand that . . .

- ☐ *Fractions always show a part-to-whole relationship.*
- ☐ *Many representations can be used to model, make sense of, and solve fractional situations.*
- ☐ *Any value can be represented in infinite equivalent ways. Most algorithms for operations with rational numbers use equivalence to transform calculations into simpler ones.*
- ☐ *Only things that are alike can be added and subtracted.*
- ☐ *Multiplication can be considered repeated addition, groups with same quantities, and the creation of area. However, only the creation of area is applicable with multiplication of fractions.*
- ☐ *Many situations in the world do not involve whole numbers and are represented and solved with fractions.*

Figure 1.7: Example of Understandings in a unit-planning template.

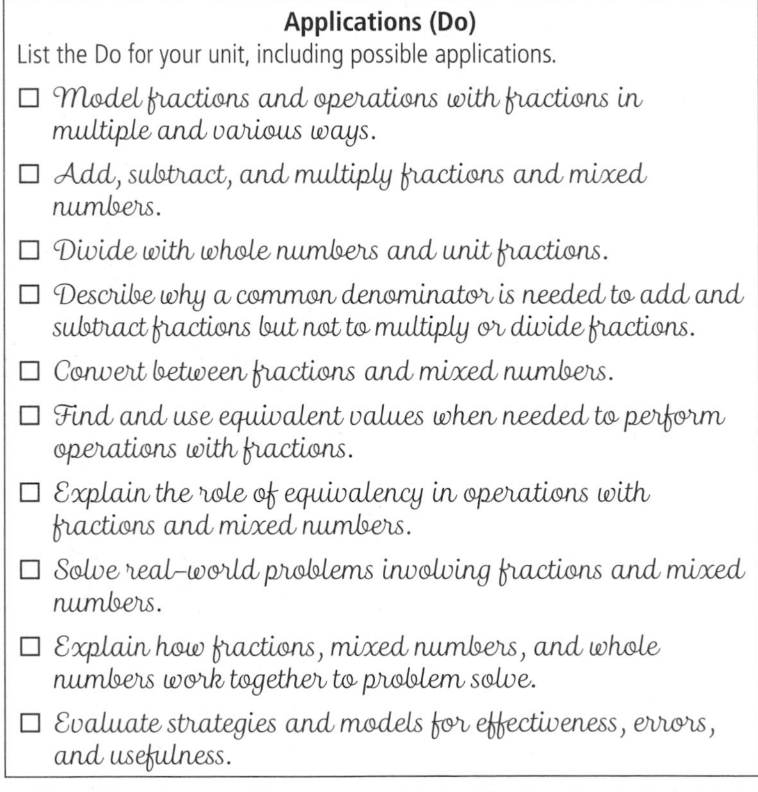

Applications (Do)

List the Do for your unit, including possible applications.

- ☐ *Model fractions and operations with fractions in multiple and various ways.*
- ☐ *Add, subtract, and multiply fractions and mixed numbers.*
- ☐ *Divide with whole numbers and unit fractions.*
- ☐ *Describe why a common denominator is needed to add and subtract fractions but not to multiply or divide fractions.*
- ☐ *Convert between fractions and mixed numbers.*
- ☐ *Find and use equivalent values when needed to perform operations with fractions.*
- ☐ *Explain the role of equivalency in operations with fractions and mixed numbers.*
- ☐ *Solve real-world problems involving fractions and mixed numbers.*
- ☐ *Explain how fractions, mixed numbers, and whole numbers work together to problem solve.*
- ☐ *Evaluate strategies and models for effectiveness, errors, and usefulness.*

Figure 1.8: Example of Dos in a unit-planning template.

Working as a Singleton

Working as a schoolwide systems team means promoting effective communications around five universal skills of learning.

1. Reading
2. Writing
3. Number sense
4. English language
5. Social and academic behaviors

Without these skills, students' educational experiences will be cut short, and they will be among the adult populations who statistically have been left behind.

We fully believe that teachers should engage with colleagues to do the hard work of curriculum planning to ensure these skills. There are thousands of small districts whose teachers do not have the luxury of waging these conversations with others in their grade level or content area. We refer to the many teachers without a collaborative team to work with, or who are the only teachers of their grade levels or courses as *singletons.* In schools that do not have grade-alike or job-alike colleagues or collaborative teams for teachers to determine priority standards with, there are ways singletons can still do this important work to determine the essential knowledge and skills students need. Following are four ways for singletons to begin with the exact same intention of gaining clarity on the standards and committing to follow through, even though their team configuration may look different than many (Ferriter, 2015).

1. Teachers across the board select common skills (such as literacy or numeracy) as a school focus. They may not teach the same content or students, but they can spell out the expectations in every course and grade level. Questions and prompts they may consider include the following.
    - Where do we introduce, maintain, and master each of the skills in each of our classrooms?
    - What strategies can we teach consistently across the grade levels for the purposes of intervention, enrichment, and differentiation (see chapters 3–5)?

Standards for Lesson (From Unit Plan)

5.NF.1 *Add and subtract fractions with unlike denominators (including mixed numbers) by replacing given fractions with equivalent fractions in such a way as to produce an equivalent sum or difference of fractions with like denominators. For example,* $\frac{2}{3} + \frac{5}{4} = \frac{8}{12} + \frac{15}{12} = \frac{23}{12}$. *(In general,* $\frac{a}{b} + \frac{c}{d} = \frac{(ad + bc)}{bd}$.*)*

KUD for Lesson (From Unit Plan)

Know:

- ☐ *How to model fractions*
- ☐ *Numerators always represent the number of parts of a whole that are selected, and denominators represent the number of total parts in the whole.*
- ☐ *Methods for finding common denominators*
- ☐ *Strategies to add and subtract fractions*

Understand:

- ☐ *Only things that are alike can be added and subtracted.*
- ☐ *Any value can be represented in infinitely many equivalent ways.*
- ☐ *Many representations can be used to model, make sense of, and solve fractional situations.*

Do:

- ☐ *Model fractions and operations with fractions in multiple various ways.*
- ☐ *Add and subtract fractions, including finding common denominators.*
- ☐ *Describe why a common denominator is needed to add and subtract fractions.*

Source for Standard: NGA & CCSSO, 2010b.

Figure 1.9: Example of standards and KUD in a lesson-planning template.

- Based on the district's standards document, what kinds of writing do we expect of our students at each grade level (see this chapter)?
- What scoring rubrics can provide a consistent structure to scaffold both reading and writing skills in K–12 (see chapter 6)?
- What opportunities are we giving students to receive differentiated skill instruction to meet the diverse needs of our K–12 students (see chapter 4)?
- How might we configure our instructional delivery differently to provide for students who need flexible grouping opportunities in K–12 (see chapters 3 and 4)?
- Are there ways to store student works of writing from grade to grade so that students have the opportunity to return to an original work or task and develop it further throughout K–12?

2. Work vertically as a grade band to establish priority and supporting standards. Then write assessments as a team to ensure skills scaffold up and down the grade bands.
3. Consider a learning project at the elementary, middle school, or high school level in all content areas. For example, in a schoolwide project on caring for our environment, each grade level chooses a specific part within this major theme. Questions and prompts teachers may consider together include the following.
    - What expectations will we have for the project?
    - How will students collect information?

- What options can we create for students to exhibit what they know about the environment?
- How might we provide multiple electronic opportunities for students to create a capstone event with another grade level or an older study buddy focused on our theme? Could we have rotating stations where students could gain exposure to electronic tools like Prezi (www.prezi.com), procon.org, Shmoop (www.shmoop.com), Padlet (https://padlet.com), iMovie (www.apple.com/mac/imovie), Edulastic (www.edulastic.com), CommonLit (www.commonlit.org), and so on, with students working at the stations according to their skills and interests?

4. Other considerations for singleton teams to explore in K–12 include:
   - Habits of mind (see www.artcostacentre.com/html/habits.htm)
   - Critical thinking and analytical skills across the grade levels (see Critical and Analytical Thinking Skills, n.d.)
   - 21st century learner preparation (see Potter, Whitener, & Sikorsky, 2016; Richardson, 2013)

There are concerns for both large and small districts in the development of a guaranteed and viable curriculum. In larger districts, achieving systems thinking takes longer because it involves reaching numerous teachers and schools. Smaller schools clearly have an advantage to create curriculum fidelity in a shorter time and with greater continuity due to the smaller populations they have to reach. The key is to be solution oriented and pursue discussions as schoolwide decision makers on behalf of students. Change the *what ifs* to *let's considers*. Teachers should remember that there is no perfect answer—concentrate on the things you *can* do, and leave behind what you can't.

Conclusion

Designing powerful learning opportunities for students begins with a unit focus and determining the essential learning for the unit based on the standards. Teachers can accomplish this by working collaboratively to prioritize the standards and then unpacking the standards in terms of what students need to know, understand, and do.

The Takeaways

In order to plan purposefully, consider the following points.

- Begin with a unit focus before a lesson focus and with your standards in mind.
- Prioritize standards through the lens of teacher input, endurance, readiness, leverage, and testing mandates.
- Unpack your standards in terms of what students should know, understand, and do.
- Work in a team whenever possible.
- Use the unit- and lesson-planning templates.

Questions for Expectations and Rigor

On a scale of 1–5 (1 is low; 5 is high), where is your school in terms of establishing fidelity to the learning expectations for preK–12 students? Are you snorkeling or deep-sea diving? Consider the following four questions.

1. Do all grade-level teams and departments see with the same lens the importance of prioritizing standards?
2. What conversations have the teachers in your school had around providing varying degrees of rigor?
3. What will you do to make the standards picture clearer for your students?
4. Respond to the following statements.
    - In order for students to learn at high levels, they have to be taught at high levels.
    - Most schools don't have a scheduling problem; they have a targeting problem.

CHAPTER 2

LAUNCHING LESSONS AND STARTING THE UNIT

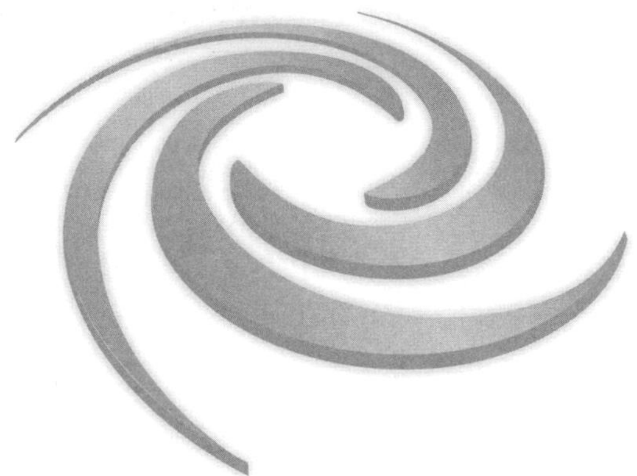

We teachers often have set routines for how we begin our classes or content sections. Does the following scenario sound familiar?

"Good morning, everyone!" Ms. Asbury greets her class. "Your warm-up is on the board. Please get out your journals and work on the warm-up while I take attendance."

Most of the students begin working on the warm-up, some students still fiddle with their backpacks and books, others continue their conversations about the TV shows they watched the night before, one student has his head down on his desk, and a few are staring forward with nothing on their desks.

Ms. Asbury completes the necessary administrative details, looks up, and wonders how to get everyone on task. "All right," she says. "Who wants to answer number one?"

Some of us begin with a warm-up or review of any assigned homework. Others dive right into the new learning. How we start a lesson makes a difference. Our decisions about how we launch lessons must be as thoughtful as the activities, modeling, and assessments we will give throughout the lesson. Launching the lesson should hook students into the learning to come, connect to prior learning and experiences, and foresee the lesson or lessons ahead. In order to effectively launch a lesson, we need to establish its focus and write learning targets, understand factors that influence a launch's success, and dedicate time to purposefully designing and implementing the launch.

Writing Focused Learning Targets for the Lesson

Determining a lesson's focus is the first step in planning its launch. It is the answer to the question, "Why do we have to learn this?" It clarifies the relevance of the learning goals for students and allows us to write and be able to explain to students the learning goals in *student-friendly language*. Imagine an athlete training for the Olympics but not knowing what specific goal they must reach in order to qualify! No one—whether they are Olympic hopefuls or students in our classrooms—can hit a target they do not know or cannot see. The focus for the individual lesson needs to come directly from the unit plan and the lesson KUD that resulted from unpacking the unit's standards. Using the lesson- and unit-planning templates allows the goals to become clear and focused. When selecting the focus for a specific lesson, you will choose which understanding (U) is being addressed, which of the specific knows (K) will be learned, and which of the skills students should be more equipped to do (D) by the end of the lesson. For example, from the KUD mathematics example on unit rates in chapter 1 (see figure 1.5, page 14), a lesson focus might be the *understanding* that a unit rate determines a base rate from which comparisons and predictions are made, and students will come to *know* the key vocabulary of unit rates and how to find a unit rate, and will then be able to find unit rates in multiple contexts. These items are selected from the unit plan and would be used for the specific lesson plan.

Many districts or schools require teachers to post some form of learning target or objective on their boards each day in order to show students what they are learning in class. Some may require a specific form, and others ask for the standard or an agenda. There is no single correct way to write a learning target in student-friendly language, but there are non-negotiable elements in writing effective ones. First and foremost, the target needs to be about the content students will *learn*, not the task or assignment they will do (Fisher & Frey, 2015). It is imperative that you write learning targets based on the learning rather than based on the activity. In other words, remember to write the target *before* planning the activity. Figure 2.1 provides examples of weak versus improved learning targets.

<table>
<tr><td colspan="2">ELA standard: Describe characters in a story (e.g., their traits, motivations, or feelings) and explain how their actions contribute to the sequence of events (RL.3.3; NGA & CCSSO, 2010a).</td></tr>
<tr><th>Weak Target</th><th>Improved Target</th></tr>
<tr><td>Make a storyboard of one of the characters in our story, showing how he or she is involved in the plot.

Note: This target is based on an activity, not on the standard. The activity is one method by which students can describe characters, but the learning target should be about traits of the characters, not the storyboard.</td><td>Trace the actions of one of the characters in the story. Why does your character act the way he or she does? How do your character's actions move the plot forward?

Note: This improved learning target does not give a specific format or task. It focuses on characterization and how characters affect plot.</td></tr>
<tr><td colspan="2">Mathematics standard: Compute unit rates associated with ratios of fractions, including ratios of lengths, areas, and other quantities measured in like or different units (7.RPA.1; NGA & CCSSO, 2010b).</td></tr>
<tr><th>Weak Target</th><th>Improved Target</th></tr>
<tr><td>Calculate unit rates in given word problems and use them to comparison shop.

Note: This learning target is a description of the task students will complete in class, but not what they should actually be learning.</td><td>Describe the usefulness of unit rates in the real world. Determine how they are best found and used in various situations.

Note: This improved learning target has students reflect on the role of unit rates and how they are best calculated in multiple situations. Students will not only be calculating unit rates but explaining thinking and comparing contextual situations.</td></tr>
<tr><td colspan="2">Social studies standard: Compare the point of view of two or more authors for how they treat the same or similar topics, including which details they include and emphasize in their respective accounts (RH.9-10.6; NGA & CCSSO, 2010a).</td></tr>
<tr><th>Weak Target</th><th>Improved Target</th></tr>
<tr><td>Use a Venn diagram to compare and contrast two or three articles on a current event of your choice.

Note: This learning target is focused on the Venn diagram and not on the specific treatment and point of view of different authors on the same topic.</td><td>Determine the role of perspective and bias in different treatments of a topic. Explain how an author's perspective impacts the details he or she includes and arguments he or she makes.

Note: This improved learning target focuses students' attention on why authors will treat the same or similar topic in different manners. It focuses students on perspective and detail.</td></tr>
</table>

Science standard: Develop models to describe that organisms have unique and diverse life cycles but all have in common birth, growth, reproduction, and death (3-LS1-1; NGSS Lead States, 2013).	
Weak Target	**Improved Target**
Complete a diagram of the life cycle of a butterfly. Note: This learning target does not address the essence of the standard but instead addresses the life cycle of a specific organism that has been studied.	Create a diagram of a general life cycle for any living organism. Choose two different living organisms we have studied or with which you are familiar. Illustrate how the same aspects of a life cycle remain exactly the same for each, and how there are also some differences. Note: This improved learning target addresses the content standard by comparing life cycles of two or more living organisms and showing the commonalities and differences. This is generalized for any living organisms, which more appropriately addresses the standard's content.

Figure 2.1: Improving learning targets.

Improving a learning target to focus on content learning rather than a task is the first step in focusing a lesson for students' understanding. Content learning is not the only learning within a lesson, however. Teachers may want to write additional language or social targets, as well. *Language targets* provide students with expectations for specific academic vocabulary, language structures, or usage. *Social targets* reflect the behavior expectations for the lesson—for example, *Work collaboratively with each member contributing equally to the final product.* Teachers can combine these three target types (learning, language, and social) into a compound target or keep them as separate targets. Figure 2.2 gives further examples of adding a language and social target to the previous targets in figure 2.1.

ELA standard: Describe characters in a story (e.g., their traits, motivations, or feelings) and explain how their actions contribute to the sequence of events (RL.3.3; NGA & CCSSO, 2010a).	
Original Target	**Revised Target**
Trace the actions of one of the characters in the story. Why does your character act the way he or she does? How do your character's actions move the plot forward?	Use the language of the author to trace the actions of one of the characters in the story. Why does your character act the way he or she does? How do your character's actions move the plot forward? Work collaboratively to compare your findings with a peer who traced a different character. Note: This target adds a language target by having students use the language of the author, and it adds a social target by having students pair and compare their findings of different characters.
Mathematics standard: Compute unit rates associated with ratios of fractions, including ratios of lengths, areas, and other quantities measured in like or different units (7.RPA.1; NGA & CCSSO, 2010b).	
Original Target	**Revised Target**
Describe the usefulness of unit rates in the real world. Determine how they are best found and used in various situations.	Statisticians make comparisons and predictions of common events using rates and unit rates. As a small group of statisticians, describe the usefulness of unit rates in the real world using mathematical vocabulary. Determine how they are best found and used in various situations. Your team will work cooperatively, with each member taking the lead for one specific situation. Note: This target adds a language target by challenging students to use the language of statisticians and precise mathematical vocabulary, and it adds a social target by having students work in teams with rotating leadership.

Figure 2.2: Learning, language, and social targets.

continued →

Social studies standard: Compare the point of view of two or more authors for how they treat the same or similar topics, including which details they include and emphasize in their respective accounts (RH.9-10.6; NGA & CCSSO, 2010a).	
Original Target	**Revised Target**
Determine the role of perspective and bias in different treatments of a topic. Explain how an author's perspective impacts the details he or she includes and arguments he or she makes.	With a partner or two, determine the role of perspective and bias in different treatments of a topic. Explain how an author's perspective impacts the details he or she includes and arguments he or she makes. Present your conclusions, being mindful of using the specific vocabulary of the topic. Note: This target adds a language target by reminding students to be mindful of the vocabulary of the topic, and it adds a social target by having students work collaboratively in pairs or triads.
Science standard: Develop models to describe that organisms have unique and diverse life cycles but all have in common birth, growth, reproduction, and death (3-LS1-1; NGSS Lead States, 2013).	
Original Target	**Revised Target**
Create a diagram of a general life cycle for any living organism. Choose two different living organisms we have studied or with which you are familiar. Illustrate how the same aspects of a life cycle remain exactly the same for each, and how there are also some differences.	Create a diagram of a general life cycle for any living organism. Choose living organisms we have studied or with which you are familiar to illustrate the commonalities as well as unique aspects of their life cycles. Compare your organism with a friend's organism. Work together to show how the same aspects of the general life cycle remain exactly the same for each, but how there are also some differences. Be careful to use scientific vocabulary. Note: This target adds a language target by reminding students to use scientific vocabulary, and it adds a social target by having students pair and compare their organisms' life cycles with another student's organism's life cycle in order to find the similarities and differences.

One other structure for writing learning targets that might be helpful uses three prompts.

1. Today I will ____________________________.
2. So that I can ____________________________.
3. I'll know it when ____________________________.

This structure combines all possible learning targets with an added component of self-monitoring for students to track their own learning (Smith, 2017). No matter how teachers choose to write a learning target, it should provide students with an idea of what they will be learning in class that day. Students need to understand it, so teachers should be careful with their own language. It is common to write learning targets as *I can* statements, especially with elementary students. For these reasons, we write the targets in first person from the student's point of view. Figure 2.3 shows the previously developed learning targets written in this format.

To be effective, teachers should integrate the target into the entire lesson by referring to it often. Certainly, launching the lesson by focusing students' attention on the goals of the class period is essential. Additionally, as students work, direct their attention back to the target, and ask how their thinking relates to the target or a specific aspect of the target. Closure should also relate back to the target. Figure 2.4 provides a sample completed template for planning a learning target in a science lesson. Note that not all KUD components of the unit will be addressed in a single lesson.

ELA standard: Describe characters in a story (e.g., their traits, motivations, or feelings) and explain how their actions contribute to the sequence of events (RL.3.3; NGA & CCSSO, 2010a).
Today I will: Work collaboratively and use the language of an author to trace the actions of characters in the story. We will explain why our characters act the way they do and how their actions move the plot forward. **So that I can:** Understand how authors use detail to make characters and plots believable. **I'll know it when:** I can explain with supporting detail the connections between character and plot.
Mathematics standard: Compute unit rates associated with ratios of fractions, including ratios of lengths, areas, and other quantities measured in like or different units (7.RPA.1; NGA & CCSSO, 2010b).
Today I will: Work with a small group to describe the usefulness of unit rates in the real world and determine how they are best found and used in various situations. **So that I can:** Act as a statistician with correct vocabulary to make comparisons and predictions of common events using rates and unit rates. **I'll know it when:** Given a situation involving rates, I can find and describe the meaning of the unit rate, and use it to compare and make predictions.
Social studies standard: Compare the point of view of two or more authors for how they treat the same or similar topics, including which details they include and emphasize in their respective accounts (RH.9-10.6; NGA & CCSSO, 2010a).
Today I will: Work with a partner or two to determine the role of perspective and bias in different treatments of a topic. **So that I can:** Explain how an author's perspective impacts the details he or she includes and arguments he or she makes, and present our conclusions while being mindful of using the specific vocabulary of the topic. **I'll know it when:** I can identify perspective and bias in information.
Science standard: Develop models to describe that organisms have unique and diverse life cycles but all have in common birth, growth, reproduction, and death (3-LS1-1; NGSS Lead States, 2013).
Today I will: Create a diagram of a general life cycle for any living organism, and a specific life cycle for an organism we have studied or with which I am familiar. **So that I can:** Compare my general and specific life cycles with a friend who chose a different organism. **I'll know it when:** I can compare the life cycle of any living organism to recognize what is common among all living organisms and what is specific to an individual organism.

Figure 2.3: Learning targets as *Today I will, So that I can,* and *I'll know it when.*

Lesson Title and Date: Life Cycles: Same and Different 3/18

Lesson Standards
From the unit- or lesson-plan template, record the specific standards this lesson will address. *Develop models to describe that organisms have unique and diverse life cycles but all have in common birth, growth, reproduction, and death (3-LS1-1; NGSS Lead States, 2013).*
Lesson KUD
From the unit- or lesson-plan template, record the specific Know, Understand, or Do this lesson will address. **K:** *Vocabulary: life cycle, stages; specific life stages for organisms being analyzed* **U:** *All living things go through similar stages of a life cycle, although specific details at each stage differ.* **D:** *Depict similarities and differences in life cycles among different organisms.*

Figure 2.4: Sample learning-target-planning template for a science lesson.

continued →

Content Target
All living organisms have birth, growth, reproduction, and death in common.
Language Target
Use specific vocabulary for your organism and life cycles.
Social Target
Work with a partner to compare and contrast.
Learning Target
Write the learning target as it will appear in the lesson-plan template and on the board to focus the lesson. Use whatever structure (*Today I will . . . So that I can . . . I'll know it when . . .*; *I can* statement; separate target statements; or other format as appropriate) best meets your students' needs.
Today I will diagram and describe a life cycle of an organism with correct vocabulary and then pair with a partner to compare and contrast life cycles.
So that I can recognize what all living organisms have in common and what differences may exist.
I'll know it when I can explain and defend a general life cycle for all living organisms and give details of differences in two or more organisms.

Visit ***go.SolutionTree.com/instruction*** *for a free reproducible version of this figure.*

Once teachers have determined the specific wording for the learning targets, they should enter it into the Learning Target row in the lesson-plan template (see figure 1.2, page 10). Defining and writing the learning target allow us to put the focus or purpose of the lesson in place, but we still must determine the actual launch method.

Understanding Influential Factors of Launch Design

While there is no one correct way to begin a lesson, choosing the first step with care will help determine the effectiveness of the lesson and the extent to which students remember the important content. Like the scenario that introduced this chapter, many classrooms begin with a warm-up on the board, while others start out with a review of homework. It seems natural to have a routine for students as they come into the classroom or transition from one subject to another. Routines that start a class in secondary schools or transition from one activity to another in elementary schools help establish positive classroom management and provide teachers time for any administrative necessities. However, students will remember what happens at the very beginning of a lesson more than anything else that happens during the lesson, and so choosing the launch with purpose is important. In the following sections, we'll explore factors that influence the effectiveness of a lesson launch.

The Primacy-Recency Effect

We know that students do not pay close attention throughout an entire lesson. If we are honest, most adults don't usually pay attention through an entire staff meeting, professional development session, or workshop, either. This is not an issue that requires discipline. It's part of being human. Our attention does not stay at the same level throughout a period of learning, no matter how hard we try.

Cognitive science describes the ebb and flow of students' attention throughout a lesson as the *primacy-recency effect*, in which they remember best what happens first in a lesson, and second best what happens last (Sousa, 2015). David A. Sousa (2015) refers to the first part of a lesson (the primacy mode), approximately fifteen to twenty minutes depending on the total length of the lesson, as *prime-time 1*. This is where memory is most engaged and students are most able to make connections. The end of the lesson (the recency mode), approximately ten to fifteen minutes depending on the length of a lesson, is called *prime-time 2*. This is the second greatest time for retention in learning, and the reason closure in a lesson is so very important. The time between prime-time 1 and 2 is called *down-time* or sometimes called the *trough*. It is not that learning does not occur during this time, which begins just past the middle of the lesson, but it's when students remember the least (Sousa, 2015).

The impact of prime-time 1 and 2 on our students' ability to retain important information should help us think about the structure of the first minutes of instructional time. How often are these critical minutes spent in a task, such as homework review, where students might be reviewing or creating misconceptions? We are not saying that teachers should never begin class time with homework review—we are saying that homework review should be flexible. For example, we have seen teachers move homework review to the middle of a lesson, and their students are often better able to self-assess and find their own mistakes based on what they learned in the beginning of the lesson. For those who choose to review homework at the beginning of the lesson, be sure to present only correct information. This is not the time to explore errors, because research shows that regardless of how often we try to emphasize that it is not the correct thinking, the error is often what sticks in students' minds, and they may reproduce that error on a test.

Ponder Box

Ponder your current homework routines, and answer the following four questions.

1. In the context of your current classroom, when during the course of a lesson does homework review occur? Could there be other effective ways to do this?
2. Who presents homework questions, answers, and corrections?
3. How often might students hear misconceptions during prime-time 1?
4. In what other creative ways might the class review homework? What are some possible iterations for homework review?

As we think about the beginning of class, and specifically about launching a lesson, it is important to effectively craft the critical minutes during prime-time 1.

Invitation to Learning

Launching a lesson should begin with intriguing students as much as possible in preparation for the learning that is to come. This strategy is often called the *hook*. This is the interest factor for the launch. How teachers bait the hook, or invite students into learning, is a course with many exciting paths. Paul Eggen and Don Kauchak (2001) suggest four general categories that will provide a memorable event for students: (1) demonstrations, (2) discrepant events, (3) visual displays, and (4) essential questions.

Demonstrations

Demonstrations are one way to engage students with learning. The best demonstrations have an element of surprise or uniqueness to them. Many teachers probably had an experience as young students with their own teachers making a model volcano erupt or presenting a monologue as a character or historical figure. A demonstration may show a consequence or hint at where the learning will lead. It may serve to model an investigation or other activity in order to explicitly convey directions and pique interest. One word of warning, though—when using a demonstration to model the task, be careful not to give away the a-ha moment of the activity for students to discover or the connections they should be able to make.

Demonstrations come in many shapes and sizes, and certainly with variety comes greater interest. Most are teacher led, but for purposes of excitement, consider short video excerpts, online demonstrations, and a variety of student presentations. The sky is the limit!

Discrepant Events

A *discrepant event* plays on expectations and possibly misconceptions by creating a sense of disequilibrium. The goal is to create a sense of short-term confusion (thus the term *discrepant event*), leading to understanding or sense making. For example, a teacher shows a surprising and impossible mathematics conclusion in algebra class, such as an algebraic sequence concluding with 1 = 2. How can that be? What went wrong? Hmmm . . . let's see.

Consider a first-grade teacher who is working on plot sequence with her students. She explains that she has a stack of pictures and phrases that show the plot of a story the class has recently read. As she says this, she "trips," and the stack of paper scatters everywhere. She asks her students to help get them back in order. Her students will remember their teacher's trip, the papers raining through the air, and that they had to figure out how to put them back in order.

The greatest power behind a discrepant event is evoking an emotional connection to learning. This is accomplished when students make the a-ha connection of what went wrong with the math problem or remember helping their teacher rearrange the plot papers after she tripped. Using art and music as a lesson launch can create similar emotional connections and can also increase the retention of learning (Fisher & Frey, 2015). For example, viewing video clips, paintings, or photographs or listening to theme songs that lead to the lesson's topic can be used as discrepant events as they foster discussion and emotions. Think of the first time you saw a picture of a Nazi concentration camp. What questions came to mind? How did it make you feel? This is an example of using imagery and emotion as a discrepant event launch to a lesson. A discrepant event should provide a stimulus for students to start talking and arguing about what just occurred.

Visual Displays

With the 21st century tools at our disposal, visual displays can add a boost to any lesson. Certainly, learners of every age see merit in using multimedia options over print, even if only to stimulate the senses. Interactive whiteboards and galleries provide a seemingly endless variety of visual options. Video clips and various websites such as NASA, National Geographic, PBS, and so many others provide specific lesson resources and connections to launch a lesson. Teachers can design WebQuests (web-based collaborative activities) in advance for students to explore and follow as they begin learning. Technology provides more options for launching lessons than we will ever be able to discover. However, teachers should not use technology just for the sake of using technology. There are times when a piece of paper and a pencil are more useful than a computer. It is the purpose of the tool that makes an impact. There is nothing wrong with a good old-fashioned printed display or using a graphic organizer. The majority of students are predominantly visual learners, and so using visual displays is an effective launch for any lesson.

Essential Questions

Teachers can use questions to assess students' prior knowledge and engage them in meaningful discussion. They can present different perspectives, address anomalies, and establish relevance. Consider questions such as the following.

- Why can't we divide by zero?
- Is civil disobedience acceptable?

- Why do writers choose different genres?
- Is scientific truth factual?

Questions provide a perfect launch for a lesson, provided the question is an *essential* question as Jay McTighe and Grant Wiggins (2013) define, and not a factual question that is important to know in the lesson. Essential questions will lead students to conceptual understanding (U) and transfer, whereas other questions lead to factual knowledge (K) that is important to know in the unit. Both types of questions are useful, but only essential questions are arguable, making them appropriate for a launch. Rich essential questions provide a strong start for a launch. According to McTighe and Wiggins (2013), an essential question has seven defining characteristics.

1. **Open ended:** They usually do not have a specific answer for which the teacher is listening.
2. **Thought provoking and intellectually engaging:** They spark further conversation and debate.
3. **Higher order:** They are based on conceptual understandings; students cannot answer an essential question with previously memorized facts or procedures.
4. **Pointers to important ideas and transfer of information:** Essential questions go across lessons and units, and often across content areas.
5. **Stimulators for further questions and inquiry:** Probing an essential question will raise other questions and issues and the need for further investigation and learning.
6. **Justifiable:** Students must defend, explain, and support their answers to essential questions, not just give a simple answer.
7. **Revisitable:** Essential questions have depth and layers that require students to consider the question again as they learn more. If they can answer the question fully by the end of a single lesson, it is probably not an essential question.

Exposure to Expert Thinking

Perhaps the overriding question in designing an effective launch to a lesson is, "What expert thinking do my students need to witness?" (Fisher & Frey, 2015, p. 70). The expert thinking can take various forms, including direct explanation, modeling, and work examples.

Direct explanation is the most common form of expert thinking we can provide students. Every class will need to experience direct explanation from time to time when there are foundational concepts and information students need to know to engage with the content. As Fisher and Frey (2015) put it, "The intent of these direct explanations is to boost higher-order-thinking skills that allow students to consider the information in regard to its applicability" (p. 70). Direct explanation, especially in a launch, should not be used to teach materials that students can learn through other means. Additionally, brain research suggests that direct instruction should never last more than ten minutes without a two-minute activity to allow students to make sense of what they have just heard (Sousa, 2015; Wolfe, 2010). This is referred to as the *10-2 rule*. Sense-making activities could include the following.

- **Turn and chat:** Have students talk to a partner and discuss the topic for thirty seconds.
- **Quick write:** Have students take two minutes to write everything they know about the topic.
- **Paraphrasing:** Ask the class if anyone can explain or restate the content in another way, or have them leave a blank column on the right side of their notes, and when you pause during your instruction, ask them to use the blank column to rephrase the content, draw pictures representing the content, or write questions about the notes they have just written.

- **Draw the picture:** Ask students to draw a picture of what comes to mind following a reading or a discussion, or ask them to create an illustration of the main point.
- **Shared pen:** Have students work collaboratively in pairs or triads on a piece of writing or a mathematics problem. Students take turns writing based on either time segments given and monitored by the teacher or a specific number of sentences (or steps in a math problem).
- **Probing questions:** Use essential questions as discussed previously to elicit deep thinking, or use other probing questions to elicit emotional responses or experiences to lead into the content.

When using direct explanation as a launch, the goal is to move the students quickly into an engaging activity to consolidate learning (see chapter 3, page 35).

Modeling and *think-alouds* are another way to provide students with direct explanations during the launch. This is the process of a teacher, or perhaps a student, who has a degree of mastery with the skill or process demonstrating, along with overt explanations, what student thinking needs to occur in order to complete the process correctly. For example, when modeling word choice and voice, a teacher might write a basic sentence such as *The cat jumped on me.* Then the teacher models student thinking by saying out loud, "Hmmm. That statement is pretty simple. I wonder if I should describe the cat." She then writes *The thin, black cat jumped on me.* She continues with her modeling by saying, "That helped, but I wonder if I might consider a stronger word than jump." She writes *The thin, black cat leaped on me.* She continues her think-aloud until the final version reads *The thin, black cat suddenly leaped on me, leaving me shocked and confused.*

An additional method for providing exposure to expert thinking is to show related work examples. This is effective when students need to identify successful work or identify errors or misconceptions. It should go without saying that whatever work samples are used are not from the students in your class and are anonymous. Keep in mind that showing completed work examples as a template that students can repeat until memorized is not a way for them to learn significantly. In fact, research suggests that much of the difficulty we have in mathematics is due to teaching mathematics through a rote process of learning and repeating steps for a given problem type (Green, 2014).

Designing and Implementing the Launch

No matter the design of the launch, teachers should consider six elements.

1. **Explain what students are about to learn:** This is most often in conjunction with the learning target but does not have to be the first thing in a lesson.
2. **Create a reason for the learning:** This will answer the question, Why do I have to learn this?
3. **Connect the new learning with prior learning or personal experiences:** This will create a foundation and connect the learning into a schema for sense making and memory.
4. **Prepare the students for how they will learn:** This could be in the form of an agenda, the learning target, or discussion.
5. **Bait the hook:** As discussed previously, invite students to the learning by intriguing them.
6. **Take possible misconceptions related to the content into consideration:** Consider what misconceptions students might already have (for example, one can't subtract a larger number from a smaller one, our solar system is the only one in space, all poetry rhymes, or Russia and the United States have always been enemies) or could possibly form during the lesson. These should be addressed early so that they do not make it into long-term memory or to show why the thinking

is incorrect. A misconception held by a student can distort any further learning, so it should be surfaced as early as possible.

The order in which teachers put together these six elements for students during the launch does not matter as much as a logical and interesting design. Figure 2.5 illustrates a completed template a teacher used to design a launch for a third-grade lesson on equivalent fractions.

Designing a Launch—Models of Equivalent Fractions	
What is the essential learning for the lesson?	*The same amount or quantity can be shown in many different ways. Equivalent fractions may look different but have the same value.*
Why is the learning important?	*Equivalency is a basic concept in mathematics, and we use it to perform operations, prove answers are correct, make comparisons, and simplify problems.*
How does the learning connect to students' prior experiences?	*All students have experienced fractions in their lives, especially with food: half a sandwich, a slice of pizza, and so on.*
What will students do in order to learn?	*Draw models of fractions and compare areas to see if fractions are equivalent or not.*
What aspect of the lesson lends itself to an element of intrigue?	*Food. A birthday party with a cake cut into pieces or pizza slices cut smaller or larger—prove who got to eat the most.*
What are common misconceptions that students might already have or might form?	*The number of pieces is what determines "most" as opposed to the size and number of pieces.* *The greater the denominator, the larger the piece.*

Figure 2.5: Designing a launch for equivalent fractions.

Visit ***go.SolutionTree.com/instruction*** *for a free reproducible version of this figure.*

Launch activities are predominantly teacher led but may also be more constructivist in nature, with students exploring the learning first, and then coming back together as a whole class to solidify and formalize the concepts. This can be an effective method as long as the teacher gives clear and explicit directions, sets the expectations, and zealously monitors students' work to prevent misconceptions from forming. Following the equivalent fraction lesson example, a constructivist launch could begin with students exploring fraction bars and fraction circles to list as many equivalencies as they can find. This would precede any teaching on finding equivalent fractions abstractly, and students instead find them by comparing the pieces that can be arranged to be the same size. Figure 2.6 illustrates a completed template a teacher used to plan the full launch for the equivalent fractions lesson.

Planning the Full Launch	
What hook or attention grabber will you generate to engage students?	*Explain a pretend argument with another teacher about eating pizza slices.*
What essential knowledge or understanding should you convey through the launch?	*Different fractions may have the same value.*
What expert thinking do my students need to witness? How should they witness it?	*Model an example of the scenario from the hook.*
When should you explicitly address the learning target within the launch?	*Explicitly address the equivalence of fractions at the end of the launch as a transition into explicit instruction. If student observation reveals confusion or misconceptions beginning to form, interrupt and give more explicit modeling.*

Figure 2.6: Planning the full launch template.

continued →

What launching tools can you employ when you launch the lesson? • Demonstrations • Discrepant events • Visual displays • Essential questions	*Demonstrations: Demonstrate how to do the task if students cannot make sense of the drawing. Have fraction circles if needed.* *Discrepant events: Show an example of two fractions that are not equivalent.* *Visual displays: Use concrete fraction manipulatives as needed.* *Essential questions: We call the fractions that have the same size or value equivalent fractions. How would you describe what equivalent fractions are? How do you think you might be able to show if two fractions are equivalent or not?*
When you launch a lesson, what focusing questions should you address? What directions or modeling should you give prior to the activity? What misconceptions should you guard against or address? What activity will elicit the desired learning?	*Focusing questions: How can you determine the size of a fraction?* *Directions or modeling: The pizza example is a good model.* *Misconceptions: The numerators or denominators determine equivalency; equivalent fractions can be pretty close to the same size or shape but don't have to be exact. The "whole" doesn't need to be the same when comparing fractions.* *Activity: Have students debate the fractional value of a slice or two of pizza.*

Visit ***go.SolutionTree.com/instruction*** *for a free reproducible version of this figure.*

From this information, teachers can prepare the launch as we show in figure 2.7.

Mrs. Francis rushes into class, saying, "I am so upset! I was just in the teachers' workroom and there were two pizzas. I will draw them for you!"

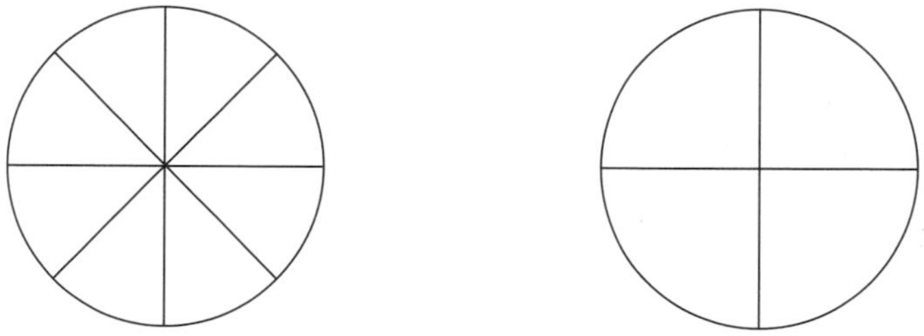

Cheese Pizza

Pepperoni Pizza

After drawing the two pizzas on the chalkboard, Mrs. Francis turns to the class and says, "Mrs. Noto said I ate more pizza than she did. She had one slice of pepperoni, and I had two slices of cheese. What do you think I should tell her?"

Figure 2.7: Launching equivalent fractions.

Once teachers have finalized the launch for their lessons, they should locate the Launch Activity, Class Structure, and Time columns on their lesson-plan templates (see figure 1.2, page 10), and enter a description of what the launch activity will be, the class structure, and approximately how many minutes it will take. Figure 2.8 follows the sample lesson plan that began in chapter 1 and illustrates these completed sections. With the lesson learning target solidified and an exciting launch planned, we are ready to facilitate learning.

Activity	Class Structure	Time
The teacher acts upset when students enter the classroom for mathematics. Explain the argument over the pizza. Model equivalent fractions using fraction circles.	Whole class	Two minutes
Students decide how to solve the argument.	Pairs	Five minutes
Share findings, and transition to direct instruction.	Whole class	Three minutes

Figure 2.8: Example launch activities in the lesson-planning template.

Conclusion

We know that the learning journey is surely a thousand miles long, and each lesson might only be a few yards. How we start each lesson makes a difference. The launch largely determines whether students engage with learning, passively comply with instructions, or even shut down. We certainly do not mean to imply that not planning a specific, purposeful launch will ruin the lesson. However, we should not minimize its impact.

The good news is that launch design is as flexible as how teachers present the learning. A purposeful launch will intrigue students with what they will learn, point to the purpose and essential outcomes for the day, and equip them to engage with high-level activities and thinking to make connections and cement understanding.

The Takeaways

In order to give your lesson a strong launch, consider the following points.

- Determine the focus for your lesson based on the KUD.
- Express the purpose of the learning so that students will understand why they need to learn.
- Write focused learning targets.
- Heed prime-time 1 and 2 in a lesson.
- Use creative launch strategies.

CHAPTER 3

CONSOLIDATING LEARNING BY CHOOSING SIGNIFICANT TASKS

It happens in classrooms regularly. Readers may recognize this situation. The teacher thinks things have gone well and sends his or her students off with a little homework to make sense of and practice the day's learning. The next day, students come back and say, "I understood it in class, but when I got home I couldn't do the homework." The teacher sees the problem is that, as someone who can explain things well, he or she has made the learning seem very logical and easy. We teachers understand, but the students haven't done the work to make sense of the learning for themselves until they attempt the homework—and then find out they truly do not understand after all. Until students do the work of making connections and deepening understanding, they do not own the learning.

There is a difference between renting and owning. Often people drive rental cars harder or faster than their own cars. If someone rents a house and something breaks, that person is usually not responsible for fixing it; the landlord is. Sometimes students treat learning as a rental, not fully investing their time and efforts in class. Sometimes teachers do not offer opportunities for student ownership in class. The strategies we choose and activities we design for class largely determine whether our students will be renters of information who largely forget what they learned following the assessment, or owners of learning that they store in their long-term memory who are able to transfer their understanding and skills in the future. We call this *consolidating learning*. Students consolidate learning when they make sense for themselves of how new learning connects with previous learning to make a coherent whole (Fisher & Frey, 2015). In this chapter, we will examine how complexity, rigor, and balance are necessary to empower and motivate students to invest in and consolidate their learning. We also offer suggestions for several engaging and rigorous activities and strategies teachers can use in their classrooms.

Determining Complexity and Rigor

Not all tasks are created equal, and different tasks will have different results. Teachers can analyze tasks in terms of difficulty and complexity, as we will describe in detail. It is important to recognize the level of complexity with which we engage students. When instruction and tasks are at low-complexity levels, students rarely achieve essential understanding and connections. This is because low-level tasks are designed for memorization and skill building.

The difference between high- and low-level tasks can be a little more confusing than it might sound. *Difficulty* has to do with the amount of effort a task requires, but *complexity* has to do with the level of thinking, action, or knowledge necessary to complete a task. Figure 3.1 shows the relationship between difficulty and complexity.

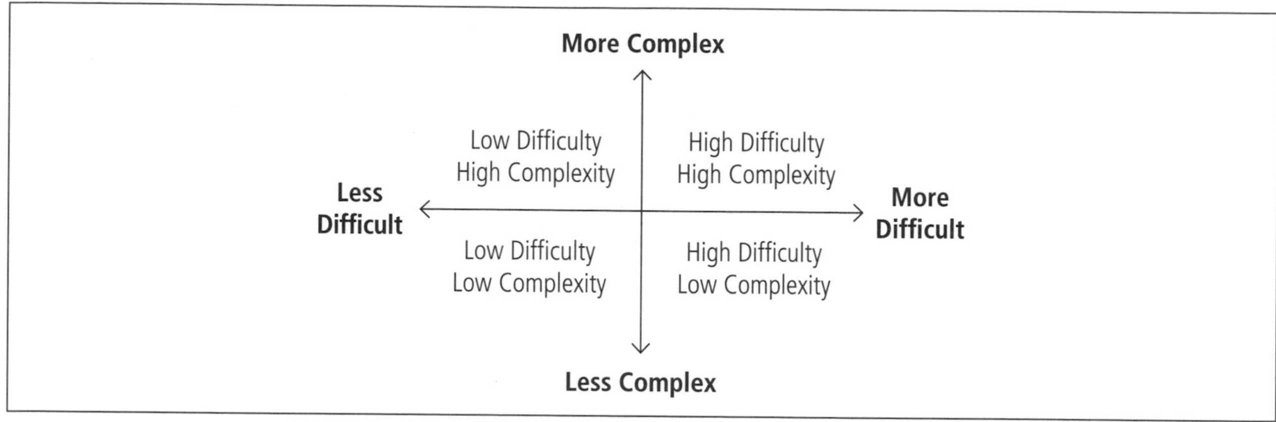

Source: Adapted from Fisher, 2015.

Figure 3.1: Difficulty and complexity.

The challenge for teachers is to ensure that all students reach high levels of complexity. It is better to have an easy and complex task than difficult and less complex task. When we think about easy and difficult tasks, anything I already know how to do is easy, and anything I don't know how to do is hard! Easy and hard do not promote greater thinking. However, the higher the *complexity* of a task, the more students will be required to think and reason in multiple ways. Sometimes teachers view *rigor* as giving a lot of hard tasks, whereas the truth is that rigor has to do with complexity. So, how do we determine complexity? There are three structures teachers commonly use to determine complexity: (1) Webb's Depth of Knowledge, often referred to as *DOK* (Mississippi Department of Education, 2009; Wisconsin Center for Education Products and Services, 2014), (2) Bloom's taxonomy (Anderson & Krathwohl, 2001; Bloom, 1956), and (3) cognitive demand (Smith & Stein, 2011).

Depth of Knowledge

As Diane Lapp, Barbara Moss, Maria C. Grant, and Kelly Johnson (2016) explain, Webb's Depth of Knowledge model is "a four-level system for categorizing tasks based on the complexity of completing them" (p. 56). The following list, adapted from Karin Hess (2003), provides explicit details about the four levels of DOK, which also correspond to the four cognitive-demand levels in mathematics. The levels are presented from least to most complex.

1. Recall of facts, procedures, formulas, or information

   Some examples include the following.

   - Read words in isolation.
   - Locate or recall facts or details explicitly presented in text.
   - Perform a simple scientific process or set of procedures.
   - Identify or describe features of places or people.
   - Determine the perimeter or area of rectangles or triangles given a drawing or labels.
2. Skill or concept development using information, conceptual knowledge, or procedures involving two or more steps or perspectives

Some examples include the following.

- Identify and summarize the major events, problems, solutions, and conflicts in text.
- Obtain information using text features.
- Predict a logical outcome based on information in a reading selection.
- Classify, organize, or estimate.
- Organize, represent, and compare data.
- Describe the causes and effects of particular events.
- Compare and contrast people, events, places, and concepts.

3. Strategic thinking that requires reasoning or developing a plan or a sequence of steps; involves some complexity and may have more than one possible answer

   Some examples include the following.

   - Explain, generalize, or connect ideas using supporting evidence from the text or from other sources.
   - Analyze interrelationships among elements of the text (plot, subplots, characters, and setting).
   - Analyze interrelationships among historic events.
   - Develop a scientific model for a complex idea.
   - Form conclusions from experimental or observational data.
   - Propose and evaluate solutions.
   - Describe, compare, and contrast solution methods.
   - Solve a multistep problem and provide support with a mathematical explanation that justifies the answer.

4. Extended thinking that requires an investigation and time to think and process multiple conditions of the problem

   Some examples include the following.

   - Gather, analyze, organize, and interpret information from multiple (print and nonprint) sources to draft a reasoned report.
   - Conduct an investigation from specifying a problem to designing and carrying out an experiment to analyzing its data and forming conclusions.
   - Analyze and explain multiple perspectives or issues within or across time periods, events, or cultures.
   - Conduct a project that specifies a problem, identifies solution paths, solves the problem, and reports the results.
   - Analyze the author's craft (style, bias, literary techniques, and point of view).

See the reproducible "Determining Depth of Knowledge Levels" (page 59) for exercises teachers can use to practice determining the DOK levels of different tasks and activities in English language arts, mathematics, science, and social studies.

We recommend having students working the majority of time at levels 2 and 3. Level 1 is necessary for basic facts but should not be the majority of learning. Level 4 tasks take a greater amount of time and are appropriate for more summative projects and tasks than the daily tasks of lessons. By working to create lessons that reach deeper knowledge, educators encourage students to become strategic thinkers, extend their thinking, solve complex problems, reason, analyze, and communicate their understanding. These levels also loosely correlate to Bloom's taxonomy.

Bloom's Taxonomy

Bloom's *Taxonomy of Educational Objectives* (Bloom, 1956) is a model used for classifying learning objectives. It arranges learning into six different categories that increase in complexity and assigns specific skills to each. Anderson and Krathwohl (2001) provide a revised version of the taxonomy. In the following list, we use the revised category names, from least to most complex. Once a team determines the different complexity levels of a question or task, it can enter them in the Bloom's Taxonomy section of the unit planning template (see figure 1.1, pages 8–9).

1. **Remember:** Recall and remember without necessarily understanding. Skills include describing, listing, identifying, and labeling.
2. **Understand:** Understand and learn material. Skills include explaining, discussing, and interpreting.
3. **Apply:** Put ideas and concepts to work in solving problems. Skills include demonstrating, showing, and creating.
4. **Analyze:** Break down information into parts to see interrelationships and ideas. Skills include differentiating, comparing, and categorizing.
5. **Evaluate:** Judge the value of evidence based on specific criteria. Skills include concluding, criticizing, prioritizing, and recommending.
6. **Create:** Put parts together to form something original. Skills include using creativity and designing something new.

Cognitive Demand

John Hattie, Douglas Fisher, and Nancy Frey (2017) explain that "cognitive demand is the kind and level of thinking required of students in order to successfully engage with and solve the task" (p. 80). Smith and Stein's (2011) model consists of four levels: (1) memorization, (2) procedures without connection, (3) procedures with connection, and (4) doing mathematics. Cognitive demand is used specifically in mathematics, so we do not describe it in detail here. However, we provide all three structures to illustrate their alignment.

Alignment of Structures

Table 3.1 illustrates the alignment of levels of DOK, Bloom's taxonomy, and cognitive demand.

Table 3.1: Alignment of DOK, Bloom's Taxonomy, and Cognitive Demand

Level	Depth of Knowledge	Bloom's Taxonomy	Cognitive Demand
Lower Level: 1	Recall	Remember Understand	Memorization
Lower Level: 2	Skill or concept	Understand Apply	Procedures without connection
Higher Level: 3	Strategic thinking	Analyze	Procedures with connection
Higher Level: 4	Extended thinking	Evaluate Create	Doing mathematics—also appropriate for all other content

Note that our use of Understand within the KUD structure is not exactly the same as how Bloom's revised taxonomy uses Understand. In the KUD model, Understand is used to delve deeply into the conceptual development and connections within the standard. In Bloom's model, Understand is used when students make sense of the skills prior to their application. The use of Understand in the KUD model correlates more with Depth of Knowledge level 3 than it does with Bloom's Understand component.

As we select questions during instruction, and, more important, tasks with which we engage students, DOK should be a primary consideration. If a task is not complex, there is nothing to stimulate students to struggle, communicate, and ultimately form a schema of connected knowledge, understanding, and procedures. We provide figure 3.2 to help teachers reflect on and analyze the level of tasks and questions they include in their units.

Directions: Record the primary tasks and activities with which your students will engage in your unit. Next, chart the level of rigor or complexity of each. What adjustments do you need to make to ensure that your students are working at a high level of complexity?

Unit Title:		
Description of Strategy, Activity, Task, or Question	**Bloom's Taxonomy Level**	**Depth of Knowledge or Cognitive-Demand Level**

Figure 3.2: Analyzing rigor and complexity levels in a unit.

Visit ***go.SolutionTree.com/instruction*** *for a free reproducible version of this figure.*

Ponder Box

Ponder your current practices for determining complexity and rigor, and answer the following four questions.

1. How would you describe the difference between difficulty and complexity?
2. Is it possible for students to be able to respond to highly complex tasks but not be considered advanced?
3. Why is it important to consider complexity when designing learning experiences?
4. Up for a challenge? Design a level 3 DOK task for your classroom.

Ensuring Balance in Activities

According to Wiggins and McTighe (2011), there are three types of learning tasks to consider as a learning sequence when designing a unit: (1) acquisition, (2) meaning making, and (3) transfer (AMT). The basic idea is that the progression of learning goes from acquisition of certain facts, information, and skills to making meaning of the learning before independently applying it (transferring the learning) in new and novel situations. The structure of AMT correlates to the KUD structure in chapter 1 (page 5). Students *acquire knowledge* (A = K) but have to make deeper connections and *meanings* in order to *understand* (M = U). Once students have a depth of understanding, they can *transfer* their understanding as they *do* things that apply and use the learning in new and novel situations (T = D).

The problem is that in light of the breadth of our required content, many classrooms stay at the acquisition level, and learning becomes about amassing information that students can recall and regurgitate, but little else. We can become frustrated when our students act as if they have never learned a topic or concept when they encounter it in a slightly different context. When students are not able to transfer learning, it is because they have not first made meaning of the information they've acquired. It is not possible to go from acquisition to transfer without making meaning. Consequently, as teachers plan instruction for a unit, they must pay attention to whether the learning activities are balanced among acquisition, meaning making, and transfer. There will be more acquisition and meaning making than transfer in a typical unit as multiple acquisition and meaning making tasks will often lead to a single transfer task. There is not a recommended balance of acquisition, meaning making, and transfer tasks within a unit (such as 1:1:1); however, teachers need to be purposeful in planning the daily lessons so that as students acquire knowledge they have opportunities to make meaning of the knowledge and to transfer learning in new contexts and situations at various points within the unit. Table 3.2 notes different types of instructional strategies for each of the three parts of the learning sequence for teachers to refer to as they review their practices to ensure a greater balance.

Table 3.2: Strategies for Acquisition, Meaning Making, and Transfer

	Strategies
Acquisition	Direct instruction Lecture, readings Graphic organizers Guided practice Videos Most worksheets
Meaning Making	Questioning (other than recall questions) Discourse activities Problem-based learning Summarizing activities Explanations Students teaching Reflective journals and learning logs Concept attainment Analogies
Transfer	Independent problem solving in new contexts Authentic performance assessments Coaching

Source: Adapted from Wiggins & McTighe, 2011.

When teachers balance the types of tasks and provide synthesizing and summarizing activities, students will make sense of their learning and be able to apply and transfer their understanding to new and unique situations. They will be able to recognize contexts that are similar to previous tasks and connect effective strategies in new and novel ways. Figure 3.3 provides a tool to help teachers analyze the balance of the activities they have designed for their students.

Directions: In the following table, record the student tasks for your unit or lesson. Check the learning purpose—acquisition, meaning making, or transfer.

Task	Acquisition	Meaning Making	Transfer

Figure 3.3: Task alignments to acquisition, meaning making, and transfer.

Visit ***go.SolutionTree.com/instruction*** *for a free reproducible version of this figure.*

Empowering Learning Through Engagement

The extent to which students develop necessary connections and deep understandings (see chapter 1, page 5) depends largely on the types and structures of tasks chosen for the unit. Fisher and Frey (2015) and Timothy D. Kanold and Matthew R. Larson (2012) suggest devoting 50–65 percent of class time to student-to-student discourse and exploration in order for students to own their learning. The extent to which students engage with their learning in class directly correlates with the level at which they develop connections and understanding—in essence, the degree to which they own their learning (McTighe & Wiggins, 2013; Wiggins & McTighe, 2011).

Ponder Box

Ponder the engagement levels of lessons and activities you currently use, and answer the following two questions.

1. What does engagement mean to you?
2. How do you recognize when students are engaged? What does it look like, sound like, and feel like?

Because we know students are actively engaging and participating in the lesson when they are the ones—rather than the teachers—doing the talking, it is important to ensure students are doing the majority of the talking during a class. Figure 3.4 (page 42) provides a worksheet on which teachers can plan the amount of engagement time in a given lesson. Teachers can use it in combination with their lesson templates (figure 1.2, page 10) to determine the number of teacher-talk versus student-talk minutes.

Directions: Use your lesson plan to determine the minutes and percentage of minutes of teacher-led talk and actions and student-led talk and actions.

Segment	Description	Teacher Minutes	Student Minutes
Launch			
New or review information			
Engagement activity (activities)			
Closure			
Total minutes for lesson			
Percentage of teacher minutes for lesson (total minutes for teacher divided by total class minutes, multiplied by one hundred for percentage)			
Percentage of student minutes for lesson (total minutes for student divided by total class minutes, multiplied by one hundred for percentage)			

Figure 3.4: Template for assessing engagement time in a lesson plan.

Visit ***go.SolutionTree.com/instruction*** *for a free reproducible version of this figure.*

Ponder Box

After you have filled in the template for assessing engagement time in a lesson plan that you have recently taught or are about to teach, reflect on the following three questions.

1. What does the template reveal to you about the division of time spent?
2. Where are your strengths in terms of student engagement minutes?
3. What next steps does this imply for you?

Choosing Engaging Activities

In alignment with the CUES acronym, in chapter 1 we discussed *choosing* the specific standards that drive instruction. In chapter 2, we explored *unpacking* and prioritizing them, using Bloom's taxonomy and DOK levels to determine rigor, and in this chapter, we examine ways to capitalize on *engaging* the student in meaningful performance tasks. It seems obvious that this alignment of tasks to the standards is the first step, but the depth or extent to which a task aligns and extends the learning can vary greatly. Structures like DOK and AMT inform the selection of significant tasks and help teachers choose activities that will promote investigation, deep reflection, and understanding. However, if students do not actively engage in these tasks and activities, it is unlikely that they will achieve deep, lasting knowledge. As previously noted, we do not believe that compliance equals engagement. According to the Glossary of Education Reform (http://edglossary.org), student engagement refers to the "degree of attention, curiosity, interest, optimism, and passion that students show when they are learning or being taught, which extends to the level of motivation they have to learn and progress in their education." As teachers, we notice every day the difference between the tasks that students rush through, possibly memorize, and cannot recall or use later (a renter mentality), and the tasks that have students discussing, arguing, and productively struggling (an owner mentality). The rest of this chapter will look at specific types of activities and tasks we can use to engage our students and maximize learning.

Journal Prompts and Learning Logs

Journal prompts and learning logs are common practice in English language arts, but teachers in all content areas should use them. Having students respond to journal prompts provides teachers insight into student thinking that they often do not get to see, whereas whole-class discussions only provide insight into a few students' thinking—those who answer out loud. A journal prompt can be just about anything, which makes the strategy especially flexible. Just beware of posing low-level recall prompts such as, "What was the date of . . ." or "List the steps for . . ."

Teachers can use prompts such as *3-2-1* for closure (like an exit card). This type of prompt asks students to list three main ideas from the lesson, two ideas they know well, and one question they still have. Teachers can adjust this prompt in any way. Other journal prompts are more specific, such as the following.

- How would you respond to the author's message?
- How would you explain equivalent fractions to a friend who was absent today?
- What causes of World War I do you remember? In your opinion, which was the most critical, and why?
- Explain the survival of the fittest. Create an analogy for this theory from our school or from our world today, and briefly explain it.

Learning logs are slightly different from a journal prompt in that they ask students to reflect on their learning process. Some examples of learning log questions include the following.

- What learning strategies did you use today to make sense of our topic? How did your strategies work for you?
- What concept from today's lesson do you understand well enough to teach someone else?
- What concept from today's lesson is still somewhat confusing to you?
- What concept from today's lesson does not make sense to you at all?
- Today we used manipulatives and pictures to make sense of adding integers. Which of these helped you make sense of the integer rules, and why? If neither was helpful, why?
- What vocabulary in today's reading and documents was difficult for you? What did you do about it?
- We have been discussing the scientific method as a basis for lab write-ups. Which step is your strongest area? Which step is most challenging? Why did you choose these?

Relationship Tasks

Relationship tasks follow a very simple format: [Teacher-chosen aspect of the lesson] is like ____________ because ________________. It is completely adaptable for any content or lesson and uses a higher level of thinking by asking students to draw connections that are not obvious. Examples and student responses might include the following.

- Poetry is like ________________ because ________________.
    - "Poetry is like an abstract painting because it doesn't always say what the meaning is supposed to be."
    - "Poetry is like a gentle breeze because it is subtle and refreshing and welcome."
    - "Poetry is like a mystery because it is so hard to figure out!"
- Functions are like ________________ because ________________.
    - "Functions are like a vending machine because when you push your selection, only one thing comes out (if they are working right)."

- "Functions are like a good relationship because you only date one person."
- "Functions are like paint-by-number because when you follow the directions, the picture comes out like it should."

- Democracy is like ________________ because ________________.
    - "Democracy is like a kaleidoscope because it has a lot of parts that combine into a beautiful picture but can always change again."
    - "Democracy is like a multiple-choice test because the best answer isn't always obvious or chosen."
    - "Democracy is like a tapestry because there are single threads of different colors, but they come together to make a lovely whole."
- A nucleus is like ________________ because ________________.
    - "A nucleus is like a recipe because it gives instructions."
    - "A nucleus is like a microchip because it holds all the information."
    - "A nucleus is like a blueprint because it has the drawing and schematics for a whole building."

One of the greatest things about using analogies or similes for relationship tasks is that there is no correct answer and no wrong answer as long as the student can defend his or her thinking. An analogy task challenges students to choose a scenario in the world that correlates to what is being studied. For example, an ecosystem is a system composed of interacting organisms and their physical environment. Choose another system in the world that can be used as an analogy for an ecosystem, and correlate the parts of your system to the ecosystem.

Window Panes Activity

This is a simple structure that teachers can use at any point in a lesson when consolidation or summarization is necessary. Draw the outline of a window frame, and begin by dividing the window into four separate panes (2 x 2) in which students fill the individual panes with words, phrases, and pictures of the main ideas in the lesson. Marzano's (2007) research concludes that use of nonlinguistic representation allows an additional avenue to express deeper thinking, hence the visual representation within the panes. The windows can grow as large as teachers want, progressing to 3 x 3, 4 x 4, and so on. The size of the window pane can be adjusted as appropriate to your students' age and readiness levels. They can also progress more slowly if desired, using, for example, a 2 x 3 window. Add flexibility by changing up the pane requirements, such as having students fill five panes with words and phrases and four panes with pictures in a 3 x 3 window, or three panes with key vocabulary, three with examples, and three with pictures. Novelty and variations in the window pane activity add greater complexity to student thinking. Figure 3.5 gives an example of a basic 2 x 2 window pane for writing.

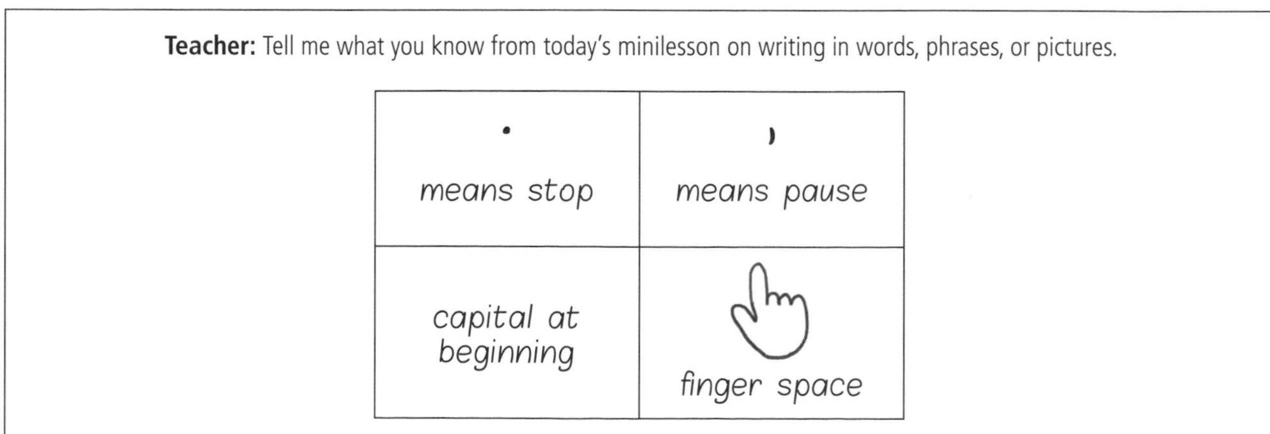

Figure 3.5: Beginner's 2 x 2 window pane.

Figure 3.6 illustrates another iteration of the window pane using a 3 x 3 format with greater rigor.

Teacher: Place words or phrases in eight of the panes, and also include pictures in at least three of these. In the last pane, use your best thinking to show me one a-ha moment you had while reading *Tuck Everlasting*, by Natalie Babbitt.

Jesse jumped off but didn't die	Infuriated Mae	Pistol-Whippings
bovine (cows chewing cud)	Immortality	"dog days" of August
village of Treegap Tranquility, mystery, entangled secrets	Are fugitives ever justified?	AHA!!##@! Though drinking from an eternal spring might seem cool, if I lived forever I'd never experience growing old, raising children, and being a grandparent

Figure 3.6: More advanced 3 x 3 grid.

The window pane activity is about synthesis and summarization and can be useful in many ways in any grade level and content area to express learning. Teachers need to provide time for the students to create and deeply apply what they have learned. Because of the novelty of the window pane, overuse thwarts the product. Infrequent use and variation lends itself to great thinking. This is an excellent way to catalog student growth in a dated journal over the course of the year.

Graphic Organizers

Graphic organizers are easy to create or find online and are useful for helping students make sense of direct instruction, sequencing of information, and organizing independent learning. There are certainly more graphic organizers than a teacher can use in this lifetime, which makes them difficult to write about. However, we will attempt to give a few graphic organizer ideas for specific types of tasks. At the time of this writing, the following websites provide good examples of graphic organizers. Visit **go.SolutionTree.com/instruction** to access live links to these resources.

- www.teach-nology.com/web_tools/graphic_org
- http://creately.com/Free-K12-Education-Templates
- www.teachervision.com/graphic-organizers/printable/56506.html

Two main types of organizers teachers can create without online tools are compare-and-contrast organizers and two-column notes. Both of these categories include multiple specific strategies. We describe a few of them in the following sections.

Compare-and-Contrast Organizers

Venn diagrams are certainly the most common graphic organizer for compare and contrast. They use intersecting circles to compare two or three different areas.

Another structure that is very flexible and adds a level of complexity is called a top hat organizer (Silver, Dewing, & Perini, 2012). To begin, have students think about the two elements they are comparing separately. They can make lists, draw pictures, or use a mind map to record everything they know about each element. For example, if comparing addition and subtraction, students begin by brainstorming everything they know about addition and subtraction separately. Following this brainstorming period, students begin to place their information into the top hat (this is the top portion of the top hat shape, which is divided into two columns—one for each element students are comparing). In the brim portion of the hat, students write what is similar about the two elements they are comparing or what they have in common. We provide an example of a top hat organizer comparing addition and subtraction in figure 3.7. To add complexity, ask students to decide and defend whether the two elements are more alike or more different.

Addition	Subtraction
Joins or puts together	Separates or compares
Plus sign	Minus sign
Sum, addend	Difference (minuend, subtrahend)

Similarities
Gives a total number of things that are alike
Uses an equal sign to show the answer or result
Fact families relate operations and number sets
Works with parts and a whole

Figure 3.7: Top hat organizer for addition and subtraction.

The top hat organizer is versatile, and teachers at almost any grade level can use it with any content. All that's necessary are two or more areas to compare. Consider the following content possibilities.

- Social studies:
    - The Civil War and Vietnam War
    - Nelson Mandela and Barack Obama
    - Michelangelo and Einstein
    - Democratic and Republican philosophies
    - Islam and Christianity
    - The Dust Bowl in the Dirty Thirties and the Exxon Valdez oil spill in 1989
- ELA:
    - Historical fiction and romance (or any other genre)

    - Theme and plot
    - Heroes and champions
    - Responsibility and integrity
    - Abstract and concrete thinking
    - Entourage and groupies
    - Authors Katherine Paterson and S. E. Hinton
- Mathematics:
    - Multiplication and division
    - Commutative property and associative property
    - Decimals and fractions
    - Reflections and translations
    - Functions and vending machines
    - Tables and graphs
    - Sine and cosine
- Science:
    - Protons and electrons
    - Animal cells and plant cells
    - Solids and liquids
    - Metals and nonmetals in the periodic table
    - Respiratory system and circulatory system
    - Levers and pulleys

Two-Column Notes

Two-column notes are an adaptation of *Cornell notes* (a structured two-column note-taking process that requires students to return later to abbreviated notes taken in the left-hand column and expand on these notes in the right-hand column and write a summary), and students can use them in many ways. The basic idea is that students take notes in two columns—the left column is for typical notes taken from a lecture, reading, or other provided information. The right column is for students to make notes to themselves on the content, such as the following.

- Defining key vocabulary
- Asking themselves questions on which to follow up
- Putting a star by important information
- Writing warning notes for things to watch out for
- Drawing pictures
- Giving examples
- Paraphrasing
- Making analogies

We title the two columns as Note Taking and Sense Making. Teachers can be creative when determining how they want students to use the organizer to make sense of information. It can be any way (such as analogies, pictures, questions, examples, or paraphrasing) that works for the student. Teachers should model various methods but allow students to choose the method that works best for them. It is their sense making that is important, not the teacher's method.

It is important to remember to give students thinking and reflecting time to fill in the sense-making column during the lecture. This will allow the chunking (brains learn information best when it is presented in related chunks versus a string of isolated facts) and 10-2 rule that brain research says is so critical for students to make sense of and remember large amounts of information (Sousa, 2015; Wolfe, 2010).

There are additional ways to use a two-column format. Consider using it for key vocabulary with the left column labeled They Say with formal definitions and the right column labeled But I Say for the student's interpretation, drawing, or example of the definition. Another example could be a column labeled Teacher Turn for teacher-directed modeling and one labeled My Turn for a student to try the same process on his or her own understanding (see figure 3.8 for an example). This can be used in most content areas, such as teachers modeling a writing technique in ELA, answering a complex question in social studies, or diagraming an atom in science.

Teacher Turn	My Turn
(The teacher models making tens as a strategy to add multiple numbers.) This strategy combines numbers using the associative property to easily make a ten when adding a series of digits. It can also combine parts of numbers for tens, such as 6 + 5 is 11, which is a ten and an extra one.	(The student follows the teacher's model to try a similar problem on his or her own or with a partner.) 6 + 3 + 9 + 7 + 5 = The student thinks: 3 + 7 + 6 + 9 + 5 10 + 6 + 5 + 9 10 + 11 + 9 10 + 20 30

Figure 3.8: Two-column format for modeling procedures.

Role, Audience, Format, and Topic Activity

Doug Buehl originally proposed role, audience, format, and topic (RAFT) activities as a writing strategy (Billmeyer & Barton, 2002), but teachers can adapt it very easily for any content area. Teachers usually give a RAFT assignment in a table with four columns, with each column representing one of the aspects. The teacher asks the student to take on a role (R). This is usually a human role but does not have to be. For example, the role might be an exclamation point, fraction, elements in the periodic table, or the Constitution. Next, the teacher gives the student a specific audience (A) to address. Again, the audience does not have to be human. Continuing our examples, the audience could be a period, whole number, atoms, or amendments, respectively. Then, the teacher gives the topic (T) to address. (We usually write the format last, so in development it is usually easier to write *RATF*, but that doesn't make a nice word.) This gives purpose to the role and audience. Respective topics following our examples might be "I'm a more excited version of you," "We can represent you," "You wouldn't exist without us," and "Why are you adding on to me?" Finally, the teacher provides the format (F) for the students. The format dictates what students actually produce. There are more formats than one might imagine. A format could be a poem, email, description, list, picture, skit, invitation, wanted poster, storyboard, or outline. The list goes on and on. Thinking about the purpose and role of the RAFT will help define the formats. For example, a video log of shapes in architecture is not appropriate for a lesson closure. This would involve students filming architecture and creating a video presentation, so obviously the time commitment would not permit this being used in a single lesson as a closure. It might be powerful for a summative assessment in geometry, however. Another option is to create multiple lines for the RAFT, and allow students to choose one or two that most intrigue them. Table 3.3 lists four different RAFT examples in chart form.

Table 3.3: Examples of Role, Audience, Format, and Topic Activities

Role	Audience	Format	Topic
Exclamation point	Period	Written explanation with examples	I'm a more excited version of you.
Fraction	Whole number	Cartoon with captions	We can represent you.
Elements in the periodic table	Atoms	Diagram	You wouldn't exist without us.
Constitution	Amendments	Skit	Why are you adding on to me?

Writing a RAFT is easier than one might think. One word of warning in designing a RAFT: it can sometimes be tricky to convey to students what learning to demonstrate. It is often helpful for teachers to provide a list of bullets to direct students' thinking and make the task more explicit. The following list contains a few examples.

- Use correct vocabulary and defend your explanation.
- Support your work with specific learning from our unit. That is, make it obvious to the reader that you know what you are talking about.
- Give at least three examples.

Teachers can use RAFT as a framework for a unit, homework assignment, lesson closure, or in just about any way imaginable.

Discourse

One of our goals as teachers is to have students communicate in class. As we noted previously, student-to-student discourse and student talk time in the classroom are incredibly important. Students who are able to support ideas and arguments and use academic vocabulary are students who are thinking deeply and making connections within the content and among content areas. Often we try to do this with whole-class discussions, but we run into some problems this way. The most obvious problem is that not everyone will, or is expected to, participate. Another, more subtle problem is that most whole-class discussions filter through the teacher. In other words, the teacher asks a question, and students answer. The teacher repeats or interprets the answer and asks another question, and another student answers. The teacher interprets that answer and asks another . . . and on it goes. The purpose of discourse is to have students talking to each other without the teacher being active in the conversation unless it is necessary to ask a clarifying question or redirect the conversation.

One way to determine how often teachers filter conversation as opposed to facilitate student-to-student discourse is through the use of an *arrow diagram*. An arrow diagram uses a sketch of the classroom and has arrows from each person who speaks to the person spoken to. Because an arrow diagram charts conversations, a colleague who can observe the class and create the diagram will best accomplish the task. This will allow the teacher to reflect on how often conversation runs through the teacher and how often students address each other. Sometimes we don't realize the control we have over everything in the classroom, especially discourse. An arrow diagram makes the discourse in a classroom visual and will allow the teacher to redirect and refine classroom discourse, as needed, the next time. Figure 3.9 uses arrow diagrams to compare teacher-filtered discourse and student-centered discourse.

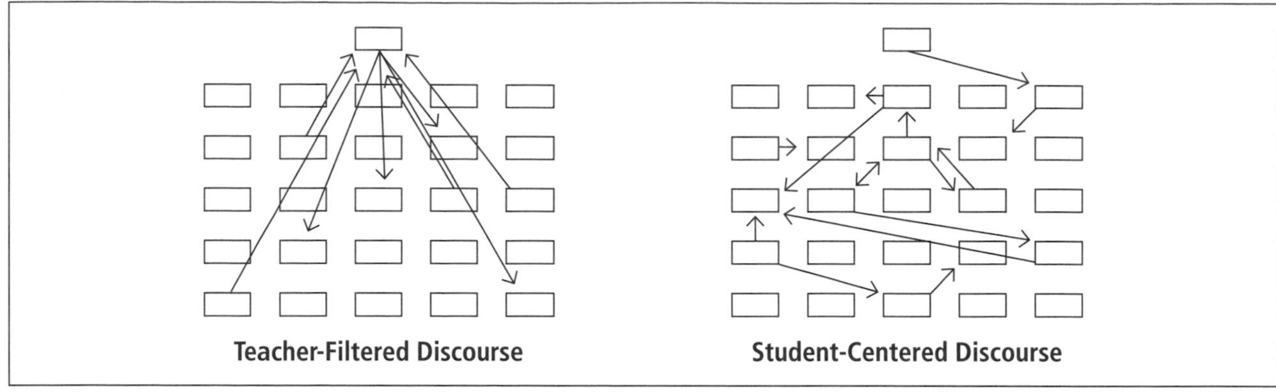

Figure 3.9: Arrow diagrams of discourse types.

There are many structures that promote student discourse. We describe a few of these structures in the following sections.

Think Dots and Cubing

Think Dots is a practical adaptation of a strategy called *cubing*. With cubing, the teacher puts six prompts or tasks on the six faces of a cube. Students roll the cube, and the side that faces up corresponds to the prompt or task they will do. With Think Dots, teachers print prompts on cards with the corresponding die pips (or the *think dots*) on the back of the card. The students roll a die and go to the corresponding card. Figure 3.10 shows a set of Think Dots.

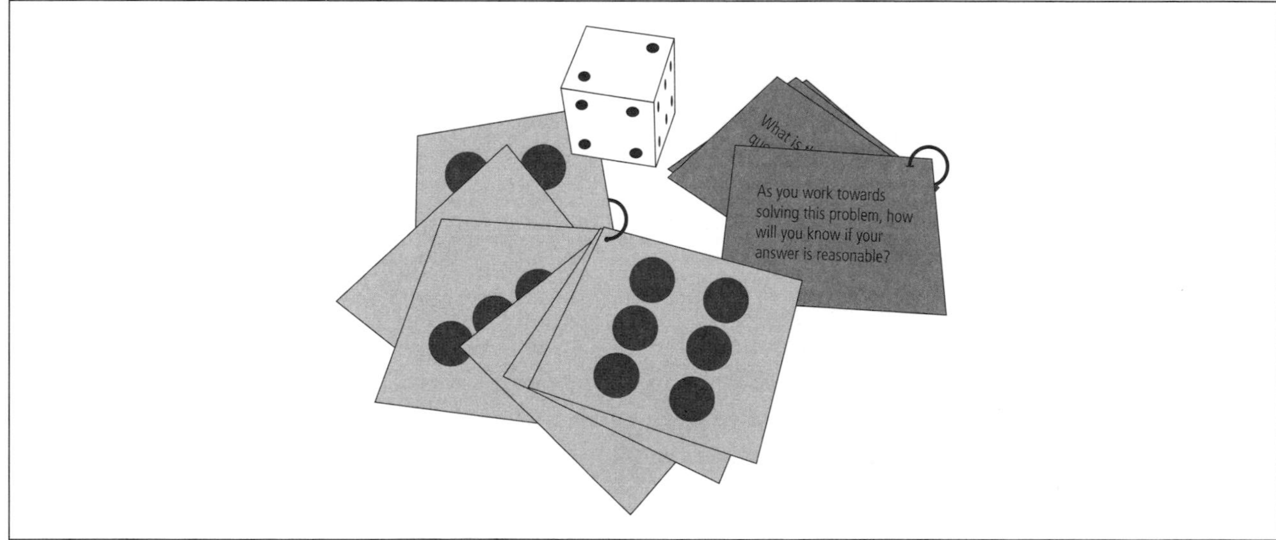

Figure 3.10: Think Dots.

Teachers can use Think Dots for individual students, but we prefer to use them in a group. Whoever rolls the die leads the conversation of the group. This does not put any unsure student on the spot by making him or her answer or perform a task in front of peers. Anyone can facilitate a conversation. Once the group has determined that it has answered the prompt sufficiently, the die passes to the next group member. For accountability, we usually have all students in the group take notes on the conversation and actions for each prompt. This keeps the entire group on task and participating with each prompt.

The key to this task is the quality of the prompts. The prompts should all be open ended, require explanation, allow for multiple representations or entry points, and be worthy of discussion. We do not recommend this strategy for memory or other acquisition information. For example, six questions from a fill-in-the-blank worksheet would not make strong prompts. This strategy is to give students an opportunity to build meaning and transfer their learning into new contexts. Consider some examples of Think Dot prompts for specific lessons in different subject areas.

- Mathematics Think Dot prompts for algebra include the following.
    - *a*, *b*, *c*, and *d* each represent a different value. If $a = -1$, find *b*, *c*, and *d* in the following equations.
        - $a + b = c$
        - $b + b = d$
        - $c - a = -a$
    - Explain the mathematical reasoning involved in solving card 1.
    - Explain how to use a variable to solve word problems.
    - Create an interesting word problem modeled by $2x + 4 = 4x - 10$. Solve the problem.
    - Diagram how to solve $3x + 1 = 10$. Do not just show the work! Model, diagram, or explain in any other manner.
    - Explain why $x = 4$ in $2x = 8$, but $x = 16$ in $\frac{1}{2}x = 8$. Why does this make sense? What happens to the value of a variable as its coefficient changes?
- English language arts Think Dot prompts for understanding character include the following.
    - Choose one of the main characters from our novel (or teacher may assign a character). Sketch out a timeline or storyboard of the actions of your character. If you were to add another chapter to the book, what would be the main idea, and what would be your character's actions?
    - What motivates your character? Why does your character act in the ways he or she does? Explain your character's thought process that prompted her or his actions.
    - Prepare and practice a two-minute defense of your character. In what ways are you understood, and in what ways are you misunderstood? Why do people react to you in the ways they do? What do you want people to know about you?
    - What questions would you like to ask your character? Write a minimum of ten interesting questions, and propose possible answers your character might give.
    - Write a letter from your character to another character in our book. The letter should communicate what your character feels at different points of the plot throughout the book. Your character may ask the other character any questions that are important.
    - Your character is going to visit any other character in any other book you have read. Explain what happens.
- Science Think Dot prompts for a unit on space include the following (J. Rex, personal communication, 2010).
    - Draw and label a map of our solar system to scale. Describe why we consider it a system.
    - Create an illustrated glossary for a book on the solar system. Use the key vocabulary from our space study, and be sure to check your spelling.

    - Demonstrate that you know all the phases of the moon and *why* they occur.
    - Prove why we have seasons. Create a way to show us what would happen without the rotation and revolution of Earth.
    - You are from another galaxy and are going to explore the solar system's sun, Earth, and Earth's moon. What will you take with you? What will you find there? What useful information will you take back to your galaxy? Share your findings with the Earthlings in our class.
    - You are an astronomer and have discovered another solar system. Find a way to tell us all about it and what makes it a system.
- Social studies Think Dot prompts for causes of World War I include the following.
    - We have been using the acronym MANIA as a way to remember the causes of World War I. Explain what each letter stands for and the cause-and-effect chain of events.
    - Choose one of the causes of World War I. What might have happened if this event never occurred?
    - You are the German ambassador meeting with the British ambassador prior to the outbreak of the war. Explain your political beliefs and why Britain should join your alliance.
    - You are the French ambassador meeting with the Italian ambassador prior to the outbreak of the war. Explain your political beliefs and why Italy should join your alliance.
    - You are the Swiss ambassador. What do you suggest at a joint meeting of the two alliances to prevent war?
    - Create a hierarchical list of the causes of World War I. Come to consensus as a group about the order of this list—that is, the single most contributing cause to the least. Defend your thinking.

Think Dots is an engaging activity option that requires few resources—a die and some cards—and provides nearly endless possibilities for encouraging discourse based on the content.

Jigsaw

Jigsaw is a structure by which students become experts on a specific topic or area and then teach it to other students. Jigsaw occurs in two stages: (1) expert groups and (2) sharing groups. In order to prepare for a jigsaw activity, teachers choose specific subtopics around which to group students.

First, specific students are either assigned or choose a topic in which they will become an expert. The students in each expert group work together on provided materials to answer specific questions or fill in a graphic organizer on their topic. They in turn will teach other students from the other expert groups their information.

Next, once all students have had a chance to work in their expert groups, and the teacher has checked that all information is correct, new sharing groups are formed. The sharing groups ideally consist of one person from each of the expert groups. So, if there are four different expert topics, the sharing groups will be made up of four students, one from each expert group. For an uneven number of students, some of the sharing groups will duplicate experts. In order to balance the size of the sharing groups, be careful not to have a single group with more than two duplicate experts. In the sharing groups, students teach each other about their topics, and all students fill in the various graphic organizers or answer all of the questions from each expert group, ensuring that each student receives all of the information.

Jigsaw is a beneficial structure when there is a lot of information to be learned, and it puts the responsibility for learning and teaching on the students. It has the added benefit of requiring students to interact and collaborate on both teaching and learning from each other.

Debate

Teachers can create any debate by posing two options and asking students to support either side. They can structure these debates by asking small groups to take specific sides to defend and prepare supporting evidence and arguments. Different groups will then appoint a spokesperson to represent the group's key ideas. Topics for debate can be something weighty, such as the social studies contexts for immigration (Do you think the United States today is more of a salad bowl or a melting pot? Is your view the same throughout history?), or topics can be light, such as asking a mathematics class to defend the "best" representation for data (Which is the best representation method for the data: graphical, table, descriptive, or formulaic?). The point is to get all students reviewing information and thinking about their own ideas and opinions in connection with the context. Debate topics should not have a "correct" answer, or there is no room for debate. As we discussed at the beginning of the chapter, student-to-student discourse should comprise approximately 50–65 percent of the class time.

Socratic Seminar

Socratic seminar is a more formal style of discussion, usually based on a common reading. The leader prepares discussion questions in advance, knowing that he or she may or may not use them, depending on how the seminar goes. Socratic seminars begin with all students reading the provided text and making notes or writing questions as they read. Teachers then arrange students in a circle so everyone can see each other. It begins with the leader (or anyone else) posing a question to which one student will begin a response, citing the reading for evidence. The hope is that students will question each other, giving other supporting evidence or counterarguments to progress the conversation. If the conversation ends, the leader may pose another question to start the process again. As we previously stated, the main goal is to connect key ideas and use supporting evidence for claims and opinions.

Peer Coaching and Rally Coaching

Peer coaching, often called *reciprocal teaching*, is another flexible and engaging strategy. Often, teachers will pair a strong student with a weaker student to teach and help. This strategy can exhibit many assets; however, there are liabilities as well. For one thing, it can create a type of "have and have not" learning environment if teachers do not execute the strategy carefully. Preplanning flexible groups for student compatibility is key. Additionally, if the more advanced students spend too much time teaching the students who have not yet mastered the content, the advanced students are not extending and growing to their fullest potential. By implementing homogeneous grouping, teachers can provide the more astute students a greater academic challenge.

Peer coaching gives students a chance to repeat learning or show how to do a specific process, with a partner following instructions. When the roles reverse, the second partner gives the instruction and the first partner practices the process. This allows both students to have opportunities to communicate the learning and practice the process. Teachers can also adapt peer coaching for a reading component, as one partner reads and the other records, and then the roles reverse. Be flexible with this structure. Teachers can have students use it in many different ways, but they should ensure that both partners assume each role.

A highly engaging and win-win implementation of multileveled learners is *rally coaching*. For the purpose of novelty, the teacher puts on a black and white–striped referee shirt and blows a whistle before introducing the activity and implementing the following five steps.

1. The teacher poses a question or problem. Both students in each pair are to have one minute of quiet reflection to think about how they would solve the issue as a solo thinker.
2. Students work on a dry-erase lapboard (or any other visual tool). Partner one begins to write his or her answer and continues until the teacher blows the whistle.
3. Partner two has the option of continuing where partner one left off or beginning again in a different way. For example, if the teacher has given a mathematics problem and partner one's process is incorrect, the partners must coach each other through the correct process until the teacher blows the whistle again.
4. One team of two finds another team of two and shares out its products.
5. The teacher gives two minutes for the team of four to decide which product to share with the whole group.

Because this is a great team builder and class builder, teachers should use it infrequently so the novelty does not wear off. Its success depends on how the teacher implements it so all students have equal voice and feel safe while sharing.

Elevator Speech

Elevator speech is a quick and simple strategy for summarization. Pairs of students work together to summarize their learning. The teacher begins by saying, "The elevator is going up!" This signals partner one to talk about his or her learning with partner two. The first partner lists everything he or she can remember, explains a complex part of instruction, or whatever else the teacher's directions dictate. After a short time, the teacher says, "The elevator is going down!" This is the signal for partner two to echo back to partner one what he or she heard. After partner two has recounted what the first partner has said, he or she can ask follow-up questions if there is time. Then partner two repeats this process by recalling the learning with partner one echoing back. The second time the elevator goes up may be on the same prompt, or it could be on a new prompt.

Ponder Box

Ponder the types of discourse that occur in your classroom, and answer the following three questions.

1. What is the role of discourse in your classroom? Is it more often teacher filtered or student led? Why do you think so?
2. In what ways can you create more active discourse focused on deep understanding and higher DOK levels?
3. What would some interesting debate topics be for your classroom? Make a list of lesson topics and possible ideas for debate.

Games

Games are very important for engaging students. Often, teachers conduct games for fun on a Friday, to review for a test, or on the day before a vacation. Teachers can and should use games as part of the regular practice involved in learning. Consider the following games.

Memory Card Games

Teachers can make a memory card game very simply for any type of questions and answers. To make a memory game, do not use more than sixteen cards (eight questions and answers), and use fewer (no more than eight) for primary-grades students. We suggest labeling the backs of the cards so students do not flip over two questions or two answers. Teachers can use this approach for vocabulary words and definitions, mathematics problems and answers, characters and quotes, historical people and their contributions, and so on.

Relay Races

Relay races are a fun and exciting game for students of all ages and are very easy to create and set up. Teams of students take turns racing to the whiteboard to write answers to a prompt, and the first team to finish with all members having written unique, correct answers wins that round. This is easy to set up if desks are in rows. Each column of desks is one team. The student in the first desk has a marker in hand, runs to the board and writes an answer, then runs back to the next person on the team and hands off the marker. This student runs to the board to write another answer, then races to the next student. Possible relay race prompts include:

- Creating representations (pictures, synonyms, antonyms, examples, and so on) for vocabulary, with each student providing a different representation of the same word
- Solving a multistep problem (especially mathematics), with each student adding the next step
- Listing characteristics or aspects of what the class is currently studying—for example, *culture* for social studies
- Balancing molecules in science, with each person balancing one element at a time

Guess My Word Games

This adaptation of the game *Taboo* is an excellent way to review or deepen thinking. It is also conducive to team building, class building, and safe risk taking. This is a full-class activity that engages all learners. Students can compete as pairs or teams within rows or randomly selected groupings. One student from the pair or team receives a vocabulary term or several terms that his or her other team members must guess based on the clues their team member gives them about the term. If teams are seated so that the clue giver faces the board and the rest of the team faces the clue giver with their backs to the board, the vocabulary term or terms can be projected. The teacher begins the game by saying, "Ready, set, *grow*!" and starts a timer for two minutes. The object is to get as many correct terms as possible within the time limit. The same team member gives all clues for the projected term or terms. If desired, one term at a time can be projected with the clue giver changing with each term.

Science teachers could use words like *molecules*, *cells*, *oxygen*, *nucleus*, *carbon monoxide*, and *photosynthesis*. Examples in other disciplines could include words associated with seasons, planets, sixth grade, presidents (future and past), topography, elements of writing, and so on. Another twist for variety is to have students draw pictures or symbols instead of talking. For example, they would create pictures associated with famous men and women in history, inventions, inventors, authors, or artisans; symbols associated with maps; shapes associated with states or countries, and so on. To add extra challenge, include additional words that the clue giver cannot use when giving his or her clues. This strategy has many iterations and can provide a fun vocabulary and content review. The possibilities are endless. The object is thinking and full class engagement.

These academic or social *oxygen builders* bring laughter, healthy competition, and variety to lecture and review. As the name suggests, when we provide activities that require a personal investment from students through social interaction, body movement, or peer competition, oxygen is being delivered to the brain, and a student responds differently than he or she would during a lecture. We know from firsthand experience with both adult and student audiences that *off-the-seat* and *on-the-feet* activities add gusto, laughter, and curiosity to any learning environment. Be certain to include a challenge to motivate students in the same way they are motivated to get to the next stage in a video game.

Table 3.4 gives a quick reference for the strategies we have described and notes the corresponding DOK and AMT (acquisition, meaning making, and transfer) levels. Many of the strategies are designated for multiple DOK levels and two AMT designations. This is because teachers can use these strategies in many ways, and the depth, complexity, and purpose depend on the specific questions, task design, and especially implementation.

Table 3.4: Strategies With DOK and AMT Levels

	DOK Level 1	DOK Level 2	DOK Level 3	DOK Level 4	A	M	T
Journal Prompts and Learning Logs		X	X			X	
Relationship Tasks		X	X			X	
Window Panes	X	X			X	X	
Graphic Organizers	X	X			X	X	
Two-Column Notes	X	X			X	X	
Think Dots and Cubing		X	X			X	X
Jigsaw	X	X	X	X	X	X	
Role, Audience, Format, Topic (RAFT)		X	X	X		X	X
Discourse	X	X	X	X	X	X	X
Games	X	X	X		X	X	

Notice that most of the strategies in table 3.4 are not transfer tasks or DOK level 4. DOK level 4 requires students to create original tasks and experiments, carry them out, and analyze their results; it is not about following a model or completing a designed structure. This is why we do not designate the tasks, other than RAFT and possibly discourse and jigsaw, as DOK level 4. Students most often accomplish transfer tasks through performance-based and problem-based learning and assessment, which we discuss further in chapter 4 (page 61).

Ponder Box

Ponder the activities you use in your classroom, and consider the following two prompts.

1. Review the engaging activities in this chapter. Make a list of pros and cons for each strategy.
2. Develop a list of possible topics or lessons that would be appropriate for some of your favorite strategies we've discussed. Choose one or two of the strategies, and create a learning task that you could apply immediately.

Figure 3.11 provides a template for designing and facilitating intentional and explicit tasks for students that are exciting, fun, and active. The intentional design incorporates all of the structures that have been described in this chapter to ensure that the tasks achieve the desired learning for all students.

Directions: For each activity, state when you will use it in the lesson, provide a description noting who leads the activity, and chart its complexity level and task type.

Task or Activity	Where in the Lesson	Description (Teacher Led or Student Led)	Complexity Level (DOK and Bloom's Taxonomy)	Task Type (AMT)

Figure 3.11: Intentional task design template.

Visit ***go.SolutionTree.com/instruction*** *for a free reproducible version of this figure.*

Once teachers have planned their activities for the unit, they should enter them in the lesson-plan template (figure 1.2, page 10) under the Engagement Activities section. How many lessons teachers should have depends on the number of minutes in their classes and the age of their students. In general, teachers should change or debrief activities every fifteen to twenty minutes. Figure 3.12 shows an example of filled-in engagement activities on the lesson-plan template for an eleventh-grade social studies and English language arts lesson on global trade.

Activity	Class Structure	Time
Engagement Activity 1: Jigsaw with expert groups—How has importing and exporting changed from one thousand years, five hundred years, one hundred years, and fifty years ago to today?	______ Whole class __X__ Small group ______ Pairs ______ Individual	Twenty minutes
Engagement Activity 2: Jigsaw with expert groups—Does global warming actually exist? How do we know? Has it resulted from how industry has abused the earth over the past fifty years, or has it resulted from millions of years of accumulated environmental abuses? How do we know?	______ Whole class __X__ Small group ______ Pairs ______ Individual	Twenty minutes
Engagement Activity 3: Jigsaw with expert groups—Does the earth repair itself? How do we know?	______ Whole class __X__ Small group ______ Pairs ______ Individual	Twenty minutes
Engagement Activity 4: Jigsaw with expert groups—Compare three locations in terms of their cultures, money systems, imported and exported products, and environmental impacts (for example, third world countries versus wealthy pockets of the world like Saudi Arabia).	______ Whole class __X__ Small group ______ Pairs ______ Individual	Twenty minutes

Figure 3.12: Engagement activities in lesson-plan template.

Conclusion

Learning is a complex endeavor. It's a little bit of a mystery—almost magical—when one thinks about causing another human to deeply understand and learn something new. For this to happen, we must intentionally design the structures and tasks we choose each day. We've challenged readers in this chapter to think deeply about what they ask students to do in order to learn, and to analyze the complexity of these tasks using DOK levels, as well as their purpose in terms of acquisition, meaning making, and transfer, all while keeping in mind the need to use strategies that engage students.

The Takeaways

To engage students and consolidate their learning, consider the following points.

- Teachers can foster increased student-to-student discourse to help ensure that students make connections and develop understandings. Student-to-student discourse should comprise 50–65 percent of classroom talk.
- To increase retention, create opportunities for students to be engaged and teach others.
- Design complex tasks based on Bloom's taxonomy, Depth of Knowledge, and cognitive-demand frameworks.
- Be cognizant of the purpose of the learning activities, whether for acquisition, meaning making, or transfer. Students will not be able to transfer learning without previously making meaning from the learning.
- Vary the strategies and activities you choose for learning.

Determining Depth of Knowledge Levels

Review the following tasks and activities, and decide whether they are at DOK level 1, 2, 3, or 4. After you have assigned levels for each item, compare your answers with the answer key, and review any items that differ from the answer provided.

English Language Arts

1. Choose two different authors we have studied this semester. Analyze and compare the two authors' crafts, including style, bias, literary techniques, point of view, purpose and intended audience. Explain the impact of each author's style in accomplishing his or her purpose.
2. What word best describes Juliette in this passage?
   a. brave
   b. sad
   c. tired
   d. trusting
3. Edit and revise your writing to include powerful word choices, and use textual evidence to support your claims.
4. Correctly punctuate a sentence missing all punctuation.

Mathematics

1. Define a Cartesian coordinate plane, listing all significant parts.
2. A jacket that you really want is now on sale. The original cost was $48.75. The sale price is $37.99. What is the percent of decrease from the original price? You still do not have enough money saved up to purchase the jacket, so you wait just a little longer, and the store's ad now states that all items currently on sale have been reduced by one third of the sale price. What is the new sale price? What is the overall percent of decrease from the original price?
3. Use pictures or models to explain multiplication facts.
4. Design a survey to determine students' favorite lunches at school. Analyze the results of your survey and represent the data in at least three different ways. Write a letter to the school board recommending lunch selections based on your data. Be sure the letter presents your findings in a way that the board members, who do not truly understand statistics, will understand your conclusions.

Social Studies

1. In the United States, our government is based on a checks-and-balances system.
   a. Define the meaning of *checks and balances*.
   b. Give two examples of how checks and balances work in the federal government.
2. People in the United States have the right to bear arms. This right is protected by the:
   a. Declaration of Independence
   b. Bill of Rights
   c. Emancipation Proclamation
   d. Articles of Confederation

3. We live in a society that was shaped by many different people groups.
   a. Identify one contribution to American life made by each of the three groups listed.
      i. Native Americans
      ii. African Americans
      iii. European Americans (Spanish, English, German, Irish, and so on.)
   b. Explain why these contributions are still important in American life today. Use specific examples to support your answer.
4. Interview a first-generation American. Compare his or her childhood experiences to his or her parents' childhoods and to a "typical" American childhood. What impact did cultures have on perspectives, experiences, and future generations? Present your findings in an autobiographical format.

Science

1. What impact does light have on the growth of a plant? Design and conduct an experiment that shows the effect of light on growing plants. Compare bright direct light, shade, blue light, and another form of light of your choosing.
2. Many predators catch and eat their prey. Predators have different skills and physical features to help them do this.
   a. Name *one* predator, other than a human, that catches and kills its prey.
   a. Describe *three* skills and physical features the predator you chose uses.
2. What causes tectonic plates to shift?
3. *Survival of the fittest* is a concept that explains how species adapt or become extinct in the world. Identify an environmental change that might cause a species to become extinct. Explain how other species could adapt to the change. How will the change affect the ecosystem?

Answers

English Language Arts

1. Level 4
2. Level 2
3. Level 3
4. Level 1

Mathematics

1. Level 1
2. Level 3
3. Level 2
4. Level 4

Social Studies

1. Level 4
2. Level 2
3. Level 1
4. Level 3

Science

1. Level 2
2. Level 1
3. Level 3
4. Level 4

CHAPTER 4

ASSESSING STUDENTS RESPONSIVELY

It was a day of long-anticipated celebration and nervousness as an anxious young man arrived at his new independent law office on its first day of business. After completing law school, he had spent months researching the perfect city where his fresh start would take place in a charming, downtown, turn-of-the-century brick building listed on the historic registry—the type of space where he had always envisioned a successful, well-reputed lawyer would operate. He decorated his personal office to reflect the high-powered attorney offices he had seen often in popular courtroom dramas on television, displaying his diploma in a regal, gold frame above an impressive walnut desk. Professionalism was evident throughout the office décor, while a different story churned internally.

The office door was wedged open awaiting his first client. Nervous yet confident in his skills, the young man looked up to welcome the unnamed footsteps approaching his office. He quickly picked up the receiver from the office phone on his desk and, to appear as if he were engaged with an important client on the phone, spoke into the receiver to address his make-believe caller.

"Oh, yes, sir! I can assure you as a committed corporate lawyer I have years of legal expertise in precisely the area of representation you need to win this case. Be assured that my legal assistance will bring excellent results on your behalf for a fraction of the price of most lawyers in town." He continued speaking loudly as his first potential customer entered the doorway.

As the young attorney hoped his artificial conversation sounded convincing, he cupped his hand over the receiver and said to the man in the doorway, "Good morning. My sincere apologies. I'm on the phone with an important client, but while I have him on hold, may I help you?"

"Why, yes, sir. I'm here on behalf of the telephone company, and I'm here to set up your phone system," the technician answered, realizing the young lawyer had been feigning success but trying not to embarrass him.

Of course, we exaggerate this story to illustrate how a similar situation occurs in classrooms. We have students who appear to have it all together, but when we ask for hard evidence of their learning, their lack of knowledge sometimes becomes apparent. This lawyer purposefully tried to pass himself off as something he was not, in the same way many of our students pretend they understand when in essence many do not.

Some of the reasons students do this may include fear of rejection, fear of embarrassment in front of peers and significant adults, lack of direction or motivation, and so on. More often than not, we see students progressing to the next grade level without the required prerequisite knowledge and skills to keep up with the content. The older the student becomes, the wider the learning chasm becomes, and the more likely it becomes that he or she tries to falsely represent his or her levels of knowledge and understanding. Fisher and Frey (2015) state, "Without assessment, teachers will never know if students have learned the content they thought they taught" (p. 89). Therefore, our task is one of being champion evidence collectors to make certain that students know and understand. Furthermore, when we create safe, trusting classrooms, students will not have a need to hide behind a facade but will rather feel free to be themselves and take risks without fear of rejection or judgment.

We have many students in our classrooms who might be great test takers, memorizers, or even teacher pleasers, but when asked to show their thinking, they resort to providing short answers to meet their teacher's criteria rather than showing what they genuinely know or don't know. Far too many times, we base grades on what we think is true about students and their work habits when actually they have been hiding behind a facade.

How do we know whether students get it? Our job as informed educators is to ask the right questions to engage students to think, reason, and defend their thinking by soliciting evidence to verify their learning. There is absolutely no such thing as effective teaching without evidence of learning. To get an accurate reading of students' understanding and to ensure that they are gaining the skills and knowledge necessary for their future success, we must first make certain we ourselves have a common understanding of the fundamentals of assessment terms, types, and purposes; follow steps of effective assessment design; and understand how project- and performance-based learning can be incorporated in our assessment practices.

Ponder Box

Ponder the scenario presented in the preceding paragraphs as it applies to your students, and respond to the following three questions.

1. What correlations can you draw between the young lawyer and the students we teach daily? Consider his educational experiences, the physical structure of his office, and then the make-believe conversation he holds while his unnamed visitor enters the office.
2. Are there times when we look at the student exterior and see a seemingly confident picture of success that in reality is nothing more than a smoke screen?
3. How often, due to large class sizes and limited time, do we make assumptions about students without having clear evidence to support our conclusions?

Ensuring a Common Understanding of Assessment

To achieve sound and accurate assessment in a school or district, all educators must have a common understanding of the concepts and process of assessment. This involves understanding the critical vocabulary related to assessment, including the various types of assessment, using assessment with intentionality, establishing a purpose as to how all the pieces of the assessment process fit together, and ensuring a balanced assessment system.

Critical Terms

There are so many different buzzwords and assessment terms that educators' individual definitions and understandings do not always align. It's important to create a common language among collaborating educators to ensure everyone is on the same page. Foremost, we must understand the distinction between formative and summative assessment.

As the name suggests, the linchpin of formative assessment is the observation and feedback a teacher makes that helps *form* or *inform* the next steps of instruction. Formative assessment measures are diagnostic in nature and can be both formal and informal. Teachers conduct them during the learning cycle in order to modify curriculum, instruction, or learning activities accordingly to bring students to improved proficiency. The greatest value of formative tools is the qualitative, short-cycle feedback feature that allows the student to make corrections while learning, without the interruption of having to score the work, which often stops the learning. Stiggins and Chappuis (2006) refer to this as assessment *for* learning.

On the contrary, summative assessment is the *sum* of the learning to date and is usually quantified by scores and rubrics that reflect program quality, instructional effectiveness, and student learning at the end of a unit and provide external accountability, as well. This is what Stiggins and Chappuis (2006) call assessment *of* learning. Formative assessment is more about monitoring student progress during the learning cycle, while summative assessment addresses whether a student has reached the desired learning expectation.

We feature these two types of assessment and categorize the activities that surround them in table 4.1.

Table 4.1: Formative and Summative Assessment

Assessment *for* Learning (Formative)	**Assessment *of* Learning (Summative)**
Any form of ungraded academic "rehearsal" during the unit to prepare for the end learning outcomes	End-of-unit summative assessments to determine what the student has learned to date followed by student self-reflection and planning next steps
Graded or ungraded checks for understanding (CFUs)	End-of-course assessments used to determine the strengths and weaknesses of the curriculum
Graded formative assessment aligned to the standards and the assessment criteria followed by student self-reflection	District benchmark assessments used to determine how students are progressing at different checkpoints throughout the year, with frequency at the district's discretion (for example, one per quarter or one per semester)
Informal criterion-referenced assessments that collect hard evidence using standards-based criteria to determine whether students are proficient (note that criterion-referenced tools are normally used in a summative setting; however, when done on a smaller scale with quicker turnaround, the results can be formative in nature)	Standardized state and national assessments, including: • Criterion-referenced assessments measuring relative performance of a whole group, with scores representing the percentage of answers a student scores correctly on a high-stakes test • Norm-referenced assessments that make comparisons among all schools across the United States by grade level and course, informing teachers, parents, and students as to how many more or less correct answers the student has completed compared to other individuals within the same performance group

It is also important to understand the distinctions and functions of assessment types, which we break down into four categories: (1) preassessments, (2) checks for understanding and formative assessment, (3) self-assessments, and (4) summative assessments. Table 4.2 (page 64) describes the purposes of each of the vital assessment types. Note that instruction does not need to stop with assessment. The only exception to this is summative assessment, which is a status check on where students stand academically at a specific point in time. We conduct all formative assessment *as* learning and *while* learning.

Table 4.2: Assessment Types and Purposes

Assessment Types	Assessment Purposes
Preassessments	Teachers gather information on how to design the road map for student learning.
Checks for understanding	Teachers quickly probe a student's learning of a set of skills or tasks without assigning a grade.
Formative assessments	Teachers help students determine where they are at a specific point in their learning, using a set of criteria and providing feedback that is graded or ungraded. Students revise based on the feedback.
Self-assessments	Students ask, "Where am I now? Where am I going? What specific steps must I take to get to my learning destination?"
Summative assessments	Teachers, students, and parents gain information that shows whether students have learned at the end of the learning cycle. These assessments are most often reflected by a letter grade or rubric.

At the end of this chapter, we offer a reproducible glossary of assessment terms (page 88) that are often confusing or otherwise misinterpreted. We feel this glossary is necessary for all preK–12 staff to build their assessment literacy around a common language that will move them forward in all aspects of assessment

In the following sections, we examine in more depth the types of assessment we noted in table 4.2. We also illustrate practical strategies for implementing these assessments and provide scenarios of them in action.

Preassessments

Preassessments can take any form. Tools to preassess learning may include a KWL chart, an entrance or exit slip, a quick write, a small-scale question-and-answer prompt, and a stop and jot, to name just a few. However, be sure to offer students an assessment that allows them to demonstrate what they truly know about the upcoming unit. For example, if teachers are trying to preassess a mathematics unit, then the reading and writing components of the strategy should not hamper demonstration of current learning. An additional word of warning in designing a preassessment is to be sure to gather information about individual students—not the class in general, a small-group consensus, or what the most vocal students know. The following list provides some strategies for preassessment.

- **KWL (what do you *know*, what do you *want to know*, and what have you *learned*?):** Students should complete this preassessment individually, not as a class discussion. However, if desired, after individual students complete their KWL, a class discussion would be appropriate.
- **Specific skill checks:** Teachers give students short questions or problems to get a quick read on the students' current knowledge and for the purpose of previewing the students' understanding regarding upcoming learning. This is an excellent way to gather evidence in order to adapt instruction to learners' needs (see chapter 5, page 93).
- **Anticipation guides:** Teachers ask students to weigh in on statements related to the upcoming learning to determine their background on the topic of instruction.
- **Quick writes and journal prompts:** Teachers give students a word bank and ask them to explain how these words relate to the topic.
- **Graphic organizers, pictures, and mind maps:** Students organize their thoughts graphically so teachers can track their prerequisite schema or line of thought.

- **Observation:** Teachers prepare a checklist of expected outcomes and, while asking questions, chart results.
- **Interviews:** Teachers prompt students with questions either in groups or individually, and students respond orally as the teacher makes anecdotal notes during observation.

An important consideration during preassessment is giving the activity at least two to three days before introducing the new unit so teachers have time to analyze the results and plan accordingly.

Preassessment should afford the teacher an opportunity to determine what prerequisite skills the students have or do not have. If the results indicate that a large majority of the students need more time to build on the prerequisites before launching the unit, a teacher may decide to take some time to establish tiered skill stations for practice and re-engagement.

If the preassessment indicates many students already understand the upcoming material, those students may receive complex questions to pursue while the teacher brings the others up to speed in small groups with explicit background-building skills. Figure 4.1 provides a template for designing an effective unit preassessment.

Directions: For each question, fill in the information for your unit. Use the planning answers to guide you as you create your preassessment.

Focus Questions	Planning Answers
1. What essential prerequisite skills do your students need in order to be successful in this unit?	
2. What upcoming new knowledge do you want to assess?	
3. What upcoming new skills do you want to assess?	
4. What upcoming understandings or concepts do you want to assess?	
5. What structure or strategy will accomplish numbers 1–4?	

Figure 4.1: Preassessment planning template.

Visit ***go.SolutionTree.com/instruction*** *for a free reproducible version of this figure.*

Checks for Understanding

Checks for understanding are quick, typically ungraded check-ins to gather information on whether a student is on track to meet learning goals. CFUs are critical because they allow the teacher to intervene with the student before summative assessment is administered. The best intervention is *pre*vention, so the earlier a teacher can intervene, the greater the likelihood for student success. Some examples include the following.

- **Entrance or exit cards:** Students respond to prompts or questions.
- **Windshield check:** Students reflect on their understanding and choose one of the following categories that describe their mind's "windshield."
    - Crystal clear (I understand perfectly.)
    - Buggy (I understand for the most part, but I have a few bugs to work out.)
    - Muddy (I'm in deep trouble!)
- **Thumbs-up, thumbs-down, or sideways:** The teacher prompts the students with a question, and they reply by showing a thumbs-up when they understand, a thumbs-down when they don't understand, and a thumb sideways when they are uncertain.

- **Click or clunk:** Students snap fingers if they get it or make a sad sound (like a trombone does with a descending pitch) with their thumbs down if they don't get it.
- **Turn and talk:** After ten to fifteen minutes of instruction, students process the learning with other students and come to consensus as they restate the learning in their own words.
- **Traffic lights:** Students are each given one red, one yellow, and one green index card held together by a brass fastener or binder ring. The teacher asks individuals, pairs, triads, or groups a question, and students respond by using the card that represents their understanding, as follows.
    - Green card (I'm ready to go! Got it!)
    - Yellow card (I'm not quite sure and am cautious.)
    - Red card (Stop the bus! I don't get it!)

  This is an excellent method to use in debate or class discussion. Following discussion, the students are asked to show their cards a second time to see if their thinking has changed
- **Stop and jot:** During the lesson, students find a study buddy and pose one burning question they have that aligns to the learning targets.

There are times when, as teachers, we just want a quick read on how our students are doing. That is the role of a check for understanding. A quick check for understanding lets the teacher know whether the students are ready to move on and also gives the participants time to process and reflect on the new learning. However, the impact on learning for students occurs through the formative assessment process. Consider making some check-for-understanding strategies into formative assessments by providing feedback and requiring students to take action on the feedback. See the reproducible "Twenty-Five Terrific Checks for Understanding" (page 90) for an extended list of suggestions.

Formative Assessments

According to Frey and Fisher (2011), formative assessment asks three questions:

1. "Where am I now?" (feed up)
2. "How am I doing?" (feedback)
3. "Where am I going next?" (feed forward)

Educators use formative assessment in so many different ways that we now find ourselves asking them, "What do you mean by *formative assessment*?" W. James Popham (2008, 2011) and Dylan Wiliam (2011) note that formative assessment is a process, not a tool. Teachers use it during instruction to identify adjustments they need to make to that instruction, and students respond to further their learning (Smith, 2017). According to Wiliam (2011), "When formative assessment practices are integrated into the minute-to-minute and day-by-day classroom activities of teachers, substantial increases in student achievement—of the order of a 70 to 80 percent increase in the speed of learning—are possible" (pp. 160–161).

In *Visible Learning for Teachers*, John Hattie (2012) finds the effect size for formative assessment, as a process, is 0.75. This is impressive considering an effect size of 0.40 represents a one-year growth in learning (Hattie, 2012). Hattie bases his finding on a meta-analysis of more than nine hundred research studies. Additionally, these results are reliable across different countries and student groups, with students who have previously struggled with traditional learning structures showing the greatest gains (Smith, 2017).

The difference between checks for understanding and formative assessment is that in the latter, students receive *fast*, graded or ungraded feedback based on their evidence of learning aligned to the intended standard and then take specific steps to deepen their understanding as a result of the feedback, while in the former, teachers gather information and make adjustments in teaching without necessarily providing feedback or having students take action. Since feedback and student action are hallmarks of formative assessment as a process, it is important to consider what effective feedback looks like. Douglas Reeves (2016) encourages use of the acronym *FAST* while considering quality feedback practices to help us remember the essentials of quality feedback.

- Fair and frequent
- Accurate and action oriented
- Specific
- Timely

There is no end to the ways that teachers can gather information about what students do or do not know and understand. The quality of the instructor's feedback to the student is critical for student improvement. Of course, many times the instructor can turn the check for understanding into a more powerful formative assessment simply by providing students immediate feedback to adjust their learning trajectory. Figure 4.2 provides a template to help consider formative assessment and check-for-understanding practices. Any CFU can easily be ratcheted up to a formative assessment by adding complexity, feedback, and response time to the task. See the reproducible "Twenty-Five Terrific Checks for Understanding" (page 90) for an extended list of suggestions.

Directions: List all of your current strategies for checks for understanding and formative assessments. Remember the key difference is that checks for understanding are quick information tools to inform the teacher of where students are in the moment. Formative assessments include feedback and student action on the feedback.

Type	Strategies I Use	Strategies to Try
Check for Understanding		
Formative Assessment		

Figure 4.2: Check for understanding and formative assessment strategies template.

Visit ***go.SolutionTree.com/instruction*** *for a free reproducible version of this figure.*

Self-Assessments

Self-assessment provides students the chance to evaluate how both their learning and effort in class is going. Self-regulation of learning ensures that the student becomes the primary owner of the work he or she does. Teachers should always expect students to reflect on their performance on formal assessments, whether formative or summative. Students should reflect regularly in class about what they understand and what they are unsure about. Students should also reflect on their effort in learning. Often, exit cards can serve to ask students how they felt their effort was in class, and what they are sure and unsure about from the class. Having students set learning goals is another form of student self-assessment. These goals can be toward mastering learning targets that are not yet accomplished (as identified by reflecting on an assessment), or they can be behavioral goals such as taking better notes in class. Students would determine what their aim is for learning and the steps to accomplish it. In essence, students co-construct criteria with the teacher to determine levels of quality in their work. When we allow students to fill the important role of owner, they are much more invested in the process, which leads to greater proficiency.

Summative Assessments

Summative assessment serves the purpose of capturing the *sum* of the learning at the end of a learning cycle, which could refer to the end of a unit or the end of a grading period. The following are different forms of summative tools used to catalogue the learning to date.

- **High-stakes standardized tests:** These are district, state, or national tests that measure how students perform against another group of students. These are also called *norm-referenced assessments.*
- **End-of-course assessments:** Educators use these data to evaluate the effectiveness of the course—not individual student performance.
- **Common summative assessments:** Teachers who teach the same subject or grade level come together to create an effective assessment to determine whether students are proficient across the whole population. For example, four middle school mathematics teachers administer the same test questions to all grade 8 mathematics classes to promote consistency, align instruction to the curriculum, and promote shared conversations about student work in order to hone their craft of teaching and provide next-step instruction for all eighth-grade students.
- **Individual summative assessments:** Singleton teachers create an assessment tool to be given to students at the end of the learning cycle, covering the non-negotiable learning targets.

Intentionality

In order to help our students succeed, we must use assessment with intentionality. Planning the frequency and types of assessments teachers will use in a unit of instruction is essential, but it is equally important that teachers are intentional when planning and using assessment by ensuring that the focus is ultimately on the desired outcome—the learning goal—from the beginning to the end of the unit.

Put yourself in the shoes of a track coach preparing to equip his or her athletes for a successful upcoming season. The coach thoughtfully examines the previous year's statistics to find out what is required to get the team to the championship by the end of the year. When we use formative assessment and checks for understanding intentionally in our classrooms, we operate in much the same way. In order to hit the target, it needs to be consistently visible and monitored for incremental progress toward the end goal. Very simply stated, we must see the target to hit the target. This requires knowing where each student is in relation to the end goal. Figure 4.3 gives an example of how this looks over time throughout a unit. In this example, fidelity to the standards is specifically targeted and assessed with frequent gauges of the learning in order to intervene and enrich students' learning as needed.

Baseline Assessment (start of year)	Practice (ungraded)	Checkpoint	Practice (ungraded)	Checkpoint	Practice (ungraded)	Checkpoint	Trimester or Quarter Assessment (finish line)

Source: Adapted from Tanna Kincaid, Bismarck Public Schools.

Figure 4.3: Instructional design and assessment model.

What academic implications can we glean from this model of intentional assessment? Table 4.3 parallels the intentional *coach talk* that athletes hear during the track season and the *teacher talk* that aids students in meeting the required grade-level and content-area standards within the academic year, and illustrates what they might look like and sound like.

Table 4.3: Coach Talk and Teacher Talk

Coach Talk	Teacher Talk
"Since we are starting a new track season, as a coaching staff we need to assess last year's qualifying records to prepare ourselves and our athletes for the year-end meet."	"As grade-level (or content) teachers, we need to be crystal clear about our academic standards and expectations so we can intentionally plan for our students to hit the academic bullseye by the end of the school year."
"With the end in mind, each warm-up, practice, workout, and track meet directly aligns to the year-end performance for local, state, and national qualification."	"With the end in mind, each modeled lesson, daily practice and assignment, formative check for understanding, and summative assessment directly aligns to the year-end academic standards and proficiencies projected by local, state, and national expectations."
"As the athletes come in next week to start the season, our coaching staff will be keen observers of their natural abilities to see how we can best condition and prepare them for success. Through preassessment, we will plan our practice sessions accordingly to build strength and stamina for the events for which they are best suited."	"Prior to instruction, we will assess our students to find out their academic strengths and weaknesses, as well as their preferred learning styles and preferences. By doing this, students will know we are committed partners in their learning and we will do whatever it takes to build academic strength and stamina."
"Prior to our first track meet, we will practice our skills repeatedly, and our coaches will provide in-the-moment feedback to the athletes so they get a clear picture of success prior to competition."	"Prior to administering a quiz, we want to make sure our students have enough repeated, ungraded practice that they can accomplish the lesson and unit goals. As students do the work, we will give explicit feedback so they have a clear picture of what proficiency looks like."
"We will chart our progress against state track records so we always know where we stand in light of our state meet goals. We will set high expectations for all our athletes, regardless of their natural abilities."	"Our grade-level and content-area teams will monitor progress consistently so we know how to adjust instruction for our students. We will set high academic expectations for all students regardless of their academic abilities."
"Following competition, we will meet with our athletes to review and reflect on their performances so we can maximize our practice sessions in preparation for the next scheduled event."	"After we give a formative or summative assessment, we will analyze student work to identify patterns and trends that will inform us of how to proceed with valued instructional time in order to prepare for future formative and summative work. Since we know frequent checks for understanding are a game changer, we will provide explicit, short-cycle feedback on a consistent basis, always keeping grade-level and higher expectations."
"There will be times when we will work on specific skills as a whole team, or as smaller, specialized event teams, or as individuals, depending on team needs."	"Since we believe in responding to the individual needs of students, there will be times we will instruct as a large group, small group, or with individuals to prepare them for success, always holding them accountable for academic standards."
"After a hard season of practice and regularly scheduled track meets, we will expect athletes to use their acquired skills to qualify for the final state track meet. Those who have gone above and beyond in their state performances will have the opportunity to perform at national events. Whatever the outcome, we will celebrate our growth at each juncture."	"After repeated practice within a unit, quarter, or semester, we will expect students to show what they know in classroom summative assessments, district benchmark testing, and state or national assessments. These serve as a status check for the students, parents, and public. We will celebrate growth along the learning continuum from the beginning to the end of the year."

Ponder Box

Reflect on your own planning processes, and respond to the following five questions.

1. How do the graphic in figure 4.3 (page 68) and the coach talk and teacher talk scenarios in table 4.3 (page 69) relate to your grade-level or content-area team's level of intentional assessment and instruction? Where are you in the process?
2. What possible challenges can you anticipate from this model of instructional practice?
3. What possible benefits or assets emerge from employing frequent intentional checks against the learning target?

Purpose

In addition to having a common understanding of assessment terminology and planning assessments intentionally, we must also understand our purposes for assessing. We come to this understanding by thinking about two questions: (1) *Why* do we assess? and (2) *When* do we assess? Readers are probably thinking that we assess to gain information, and we assess all the time through student observation, in-class assignments, writing, exit cards, homework, quizzes, tests, and just about everything that happens in a classroom (Smith, 2017). Our experience in working with teachers across the country and asking these two questions in order to frame our discussion on assessment has shown these to be common answers, and we agree that they are correct. Paramount in all of this is the understanding that assessment is much more than taking a collection of scores and crunching data for the purpose of grading.

Basically, *why* we assess is to collect evidence of learning. We should view assessment as gathering information to improve student learning and development rather than as a way to justify grades; it is much more than collecting a number. To *assess*, derived from the Latin word *assidere*, means to *sit beside* (Vagle, 2015). The student and teacher interaction is essential when assessing student work. Rather than a monologue (teacher *to* student) it becomes a critical dialogue (teacher *and* student) that involves thinking, reasoning, explaining, reworking, negotiating, and redoing. This kind of formative assessment gathers information about a student's thought process that the teacher can address before the unit comes to an end.

When we assess helps us define broad categories of assessment that fit together to form a larger process. When we assess before the unit (preassessment), we use the information to determine what students already know, understand, and are able to do (KUD), and equally important, what they do not know, understand, and have abilities in. The most essential way to use preassessment information is for planning how to start a unit. It does not have to take the form of a pretest but can be accomplished through several different strategies (Smith, 2017). Some of these strategies include individual KWL charts, Frayer models, quick writes, true-or-false concept checks, and definition checks. Additionally, you can adapt all of the CFU strategies featured in the reproducible "Twenty-Five Terrific Checks for Understanding" (page 90) to use as preassessments.

Assessments during the unit are either formative assessments or checks for understanding. Teachers use these to measure the status of the students' current learning and determine their next steps and value them as academic "rehearsals." Just like performers who practice for several weeks with a director to help prepare them before opening night by giving them direction to improve their performance, the teacher gives explicit feedback to help students more deeply understand where their performance currently is and what their own next steps should be to improve learning before the summative assessment (opening night) evaluates the quality of their academic proficiency.

Self-assessment becomes a critical part of the process during the unit, as well. It is only through the process of self-reflection that practices change. Students too often do not reflect on their own learning process and the status of their learning. They might be aware that they are doing well or not, but not *why* that is the case. Student self-assessment should enable students to better understand themselves as learners and how to continue to improve their learning. The ultimate message we send to students during this phase of learning must be that their genes do not determine how much they are able to grow but rather their effort and persistence do.

Finally, at the end of the unit, the act of assessment progresses to *evaluation*, or summative assessment. To *evaluate* implies that we *put value to* one's work, as in a final grade. Upon the opening night of a play, the public evaluates the cast members in terms of their readiness to entertain, and the media publish these evaluations in the form of reviews. Likewise, at the end of a unit, the teacher as evaluator judges the "value" of student work to this point in time. Traditional school settings most often express these evaluative measures in the A, B, C, D, F system or as a percentage. The difficulty with a summative assessment alone is that it doesn't express what part of the learning the student does or does not understand. It is simply a status check delivered to learners so they know where they stand academically.

Balance

According to Nicole Dimich Vagle (2015), high-quality assessment practices:

- Motivate and engage students
- Communicate strengths in terms of learning
- Provide intentional opportunities to learn from mistakes and failures
- Generate confidence and success

We concur with the wisdom and simplicity of these suggestions. One of the many items Vagle (2015) challenges us to consider is the balance or lack of balance of assessment types in a school or district's overall assessment plan. Figure 4.4 juxtaposes the assessment priorities of two different districts. The sizes of the boxes directly relate to the importance the districts have placed on the assessment type. Readers should consider which seems most indicative of the assessment reality in their own schools or districts.

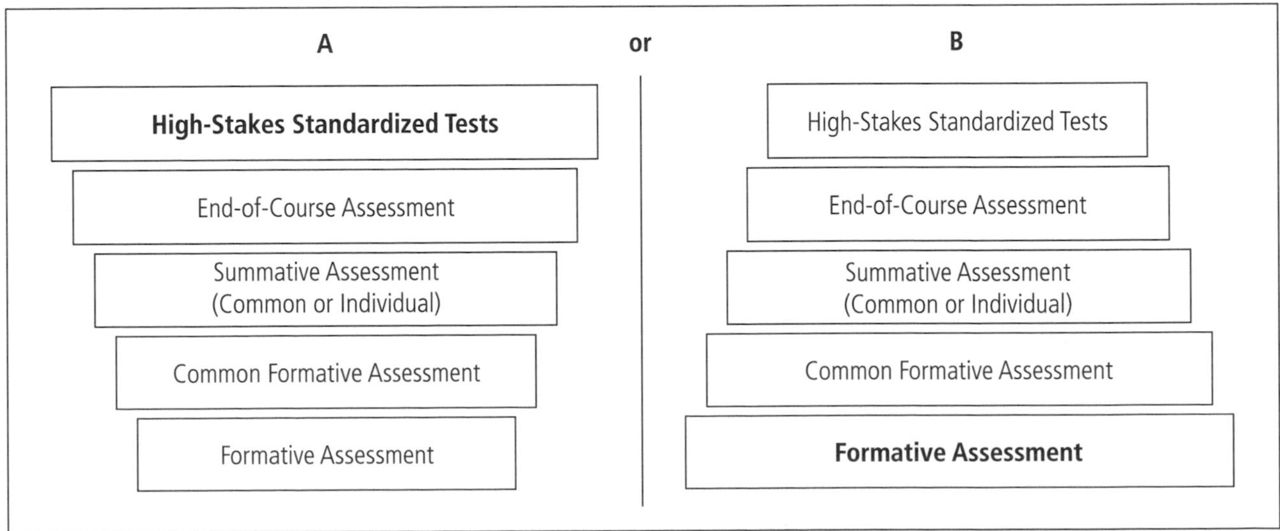

Source: Adapted from Vagle, 2016. Used with permission.

Figure 4.4: Assessment priorities in two school districts.

As represented by the sizes of the boxes in figure 4.4, the school district in column A exhibits an imbalanced approach to assessment. They place their highest value on assessment data deriving from high-stakes assessments to include norm-referenced state and national test scores, in addition to end-of-course summative assessments, which are used most effectively to holistically evaluate course effectiveness rather than evaluate individual student achievement. The school district represented in column B recognizes the many valued assessment tools available to provide a balanced picture of student achievement but places the highest value on the commonly written summative and formative assessments by a grade-alike or course-alike collaborative team. Of greatest importance are the frequent, short-cycle, in-the-moment gauges of the learning where repeated practice makes the learning more secure.

Figure 4.5 provides a worksheet for teachers to self-evaluate their assessment practices.

Assessment Type	Strategies	Frequency
Preassessment		________ Always ________ Often ________ Rarely ________ Never
Checks for understanding (little feedback or student action)		________ Always ________ Often ________ Rarely ________ Never
Formative assessment with feedback and required student action		________ Always ________ Often ________ Rarely ________ Never
Self-assessment		________ Always ________ Often ________ Rarely ________ Never
Summative assessment		________ Always ________ Often ________ Rarely ________ Never

Figure 4.5: Template for self-assessing assessment practices.

Visit ***go.SolutionTree.com/instruction*** *for a free reproducible version of this figure.*

Ponder Box

If working as a grade-level team, discuss the status of the assessment dynamics in your school or district using the following five questions. If working as a singleton, consider the implications within your own classroom.

1. What would your assessment graphic look like for your grade level or in your classroom? (refer to figure 4.3, page 68)?
2. Is there balance or imbalance?
3. What body of evidence are you using to reach these assessment conclusions?
4. Are all the current assessment tools you regularly use purposeful, or do you need to streamline, revise, or omit any of them due to irrelevancy or duplication?
5. What is one positive step that you can take to create a more balanced assessment picture?

Following Steps of Effective Assessment Design

Though the following steps of designing summative assessments have evolved from site-based work with teacher teams around the United States, Nicole Dimich Vagle's thoughtful work has influenced our thinking. Vagle (2015) contends that the following five steps need to be the foundation of constructing accurate and high-quality summative tasks.

1. Choose, unpack, and engage students in the standards. We have modified this using our CUES acronym. Refer to chapters 1 (page 5), 2 (page 21), and 3 (page 35), respectively, for each component of CUES.
2. Collect the data from an assessment.
3. Interpret the data.
4. Take action.
5. Assess summatively.

We are going to walk readers through these five steps using the example of a social studies unit on global trade. Regardless of the content or grade level, these steps remain the same when designing cohesive assessments for a unit.

Step 1: Choose, Unpack, and Engage in the Standards

Step 1 comprises the processes outlined in chapters 1, 2, and 3 using the unit-planning template (see figure 1.1, pages 8–9). A strong foundation has been laid for fully aligned summative measures of student knowing and understanding. While the steps outlined here pertain to summative assessments, recall that you can use the lesson-plan template (see figure 1.2, page 10) to design a formative assessment for a specific lesson and learning target.

As a refresher, this first step includes choosing, unpacking, and prioritizing the standards, and then inviting students into action through methods of engagement. Figure 4.6 (page 74) shows the beginning of the unit-planning template for the social studies unit on global trade with the priority standards and KUD sections completed. Note that the team in this scenario has also developed essential questions based on the unit's understandings, which are typically written after the CUES process has been completed. However, the team is autonomous and can determine when the writing of essential questions best fits its needs (see chapter 2, page 21).

Unit Title: *Global Trade* **Subject Area:** *Social Studies* **Grade Level:** *11*

Identified Standards and Benchmarks (CUES):

Specific social studies standards for this unit are adapted from New York state social studies standards (New York City Department of Education, n.d.).

Standard 3: Geography—Students will use a variety of intellectual skills to demonstrate their understanding of the geography of the interdependent world in which we live—local, national, and global—including the distribution of people, places, and environments over Earth's surface.

Standard 4: Economics—Students will use a variety of intellectual skills to demonstrate their understanding of how the United States and other societies develop economic systems and associated institutions to allocate scarce resources, and how major decision-making units function in the United States and other national economies.

Social Studies Practices

Comparison and Contextualization: Describe the relationship between geography, economics, and history as a context for events and movements and as a matrix of time and place.

Geographic Reasoning: Use maps, photos, satellite images, and other representations to explain relationships between locations of places and regions and their political, cultural, and economic dynamics.

Economics and Economic Systems: Analyze ways in which incentives influence what is produced and distributed in a market system. Use economic indicators to analyze the current and future state of the economy.

Civic Participation: Participate in activities that focus on a classroom, school, community, state, or nation. Participate in persuading, debating, negotiating, and compromising in the resolution of conflicts and differences.

Social Studies Themes

Geography, Humans, and the Environment (GEO)

Power, Authority, and Governance (GOV)

Civic Ideals and Practices (CIV)

Creation, Expansion, and Interaction of Economic Systems (ECO) (TECH)

Global Connections and Exchange (EXCH)

Suggested Time Frame (Grading Period)

☐ Q1 ☐ Q2 ☒ Q3 ☐ Q4

Priority Standards	Unit Topic and Universal Theme	Know
☐ *Read closely to determine what the text says explicitly and to make logical inferences from it; cite specific textual evidence when writing or speaking to support conclusions drawn from the text.*	Describe what this unit is about. What are the big ideas and skills that students will develop in the unit? *This unit describes the importance of a strong economy, alliances, and interdependence among countries in global trade.*	List Knows for your unit, including essential vocabulary. ☐ *Read closely.* ☐ *Cite textual evidence.* ☐ *Make inferences.*

Figure 4.6: Unit template with completed priority standards and KUD sections.

Priority Standards (cont.)	Understandings	Know (cont.)
☐ *Determine central ideas or themes of a text and analyze their development; summarize the key supporting details and ideas.* ☐ *Analyze how and why individuals, events, and ideas develop and interact over the course of a text.*	List the essential understandings for your unit. Students will understand that . . . ☐ *Countries form alliances and interdependence whenever it is mutually beneficial.* ☐ *A country's economic survival is largely based on resources, trade, and alliances.* ☐ *Industry and trade have both positive and negative consequences.* ☐ *Individuals, ideas, and events develop over time even when they seemingly just happen.* ☐ *Close reading of a text allows readers to determine validity based on detail and evidence provided by the author.* **Essential Questions** ☐ *How interdependent are countries (or how interdependent should they be)?* ☐ *Why do countries import and export?* ☐ *What factors influence trade?* ☐ *How do regular importing and exporting practices worldwide affect travel of any kind?* ☐ *To what extent do importing and exporting affect the world habitat (our physical environment)?* **Applications (Do)** List the Do for your unit, including possible applications. ☐ *Vocabulary: inference, close read, evidence, central ideas, import, export, ecosystems, interdependence, trade* ☐ *How to develop central ideas* ☐ *How to determine evidence* ☐ *Specific countries' trade alliances* ☐ *Specific countries' imports and exports* ☐ *Trade routes* ☐ *Transportation vessels* ☐ *History of import and export*	☐ *Determine central ideas and themes.* ☐ *Analyze the development and interactions of people, events, and ideas.* ☐ *Draw and support conclusions.* ☐ *Summarize.*

Once these foundations for the unit are complete, the teacher's thinking turns to learning targets. This is how we invite students into learning and establish the importance and criteria of the standards. Teachers can do this on a lesson-by-lesson basis, but establishing the learning targets alongside the KUD (see chapter 2, page 21) is more effective. Figure 4.7 (page 76) lists learning targets for the unit, ranking each according to its Depth of Knowledge level (see chapter 3, page 35).

Student-Friendly *I Can* Statements	DOK 1	DOK 2	DOK 3	DOK 4
1. I can read the text closely to understand what the author is trying to convey to the reader.			X	
2. I can make inferences (predictions) based on the text.		X		
3. I can cite evidence I find in the text to support my thinking.		X		
4. I can support my conclusions based on what I read.			X	
5. I can determine the central ideas from the text.		X		
6. I can compare and contrast and analyze how individuals, events, and ideas from the text change over time.			X	X
7. I can support my claims and counterclaims with resources I have read and researched.			X	
8. I can write a convincing argument backed by strong resources.			X	X

Figure 4.7: Learning targets and Depth of Knowledge levels.

Visit ***go.SolutionTree.com/instruction*** *for a free reproducible version of this figure.*

Reflect for a moment on the kinds of assessments you have completed in the past. When you performed with the greatest investment that resulted in greatest proficiency, what characteristics were present in the assessment? We would wager that most learners would indicate that there was an interesting topic written in grade-level-appropriate language that invited students to do, show, and tell their learning in meaningful ways. This is why engagement is so important. When thinking about and planning the student engagement aspect of this step, consider all of the strategies we shared in chapter 3 (page 35). Following are possible performance tasks listed from most to least complex; however, both kinds of complexity should be interspersed throughout the unit.

- Prepare a capstone project either through video, PowerPoint, research paper, or virtual presentation that will include all prerequisite components as the teacher outlined.
- Write an argument based on research.
- Establish a thesis, use a compare-and-contrast graphic organizer accompanied by text evidence, and generate a claim or counterclaim from the text evidence.
- Cite text evidence related to the topic.
- Read numerous nonfiction texts of choice and establish a list of facts and opinions, and a questions list.
- Make inferences about the topic and begin a search to find the answers.
- Generate questions related to global economy and form expert groups based on interest.
- Study maps, identify global trade routes, and determine how they impact imports and exports.
- Define *imports* and *exports* and other vocabulary related to global trade.
- Develop a graphic organizer or KWL chart that relates to global trade.

It is now time to start the unit. As we pointed out in chapter 2 (page 21), the launch of the lesson is critically important and can provide assessment information. As a launch into the unit, we have decided to use a YouTube video (https://www.youtube.com/watch?v=gMfrQ5su_SI) to initiate student thinking and to build context. Figure 4.8 shows the completed lesson-planning template for the first lesson in the social studies unit, including details on the launch and instructional tasks.

Lesson-Planning Template
Global Trade Introduction

KUD for Lesson (From Unit Plan)

Know: trade, import, export, trade routes, ecosystems, trade history, inference, and implications

Understand: A country's economic survival is largely based on resources, trade, and alliances. Industry and trade have both positive and negative consequences.

Do: Read closely. Cite textual evidence. Make inferences.

Learning Target:

Today I will . . . read text closely and make a supported claim.

So that I can . . . explain the development of trade and its impact on the earth.

I will know it when . . . I can cite specific evidence and debate my position with others.

Activity	Class Structure	Time
Launch activity: Imagine what it must look like if you are observing global trade (importing and exporting) from outer space. What possible effects might this travel have upon the ecosystem? What questions come to mind when you observe this YouTube video?	__X__ Whole class _____ Small group _____ Pairs _____ Individual	Five minutes with discussion
Engagement Activity 1: Jigsaw with expert groups—How has importing and exporting changed from one thousand years, five hundred years, one hundred years, and fifty years ago to today? **Differentiation:** Most basic reading reference material	_____ Whole class __X__ Small group _____ Pairs _____ Individual	Twenty minutes
Engagement Activity 2: Jigsaw with expert groups—Does global warming actually exist? How do we know? Has it resulted from how industry has abused the earth over the past fifty years or has it resulted from millions of years of accumulated environmental abuses? How do we know? **Differentiation:** Midlevel reading material	_____ Whole class __X__ Small group _____ Pairs _____ Individual	Twenty minutes
Engagement Activity 3: Jigsaw with expert groups—Does the earth repair itself? How do we know? **Differentiation:** High-level reading material	_____ Whole class __X__ Small group _____ Pairs _____ Individual	Twenty minutes
Engagement Activity 4: Jigsaw with expert groups—Compare three locations in terms of their cultures, money systems, imported and exported products, and environmental impacts. **Differentiation:** Most sophisticated inference needed from reading	_____ Whole class __X__ Small group _____ Pairs _____ Individual	Twenty minutes

Figure 4.8: Lesson plan for lesson 1 of global trade.

continued →

Engagement Activity 5: Jigsaw with sharing groups—Put students into groups with four members each, one from each expert group, to teach each other the answers to their questions. Together, they will propose an answer to the essential question, To what extent do importing and exporting affect the world habitat (our physical environment)?	______ Whole class __X__ Small group ______ Pairs ______ Individual	Thirty minutes
Formative Assessment and Check for Understanding: Closely monitor the various groups to check for understanding and pose advancing and assessing questions as needed to guide students.	______ Whole class __X__ Small group ______ Pairs ______ Individual	Varies based on task being assessed
Closure Activity: Students will form a human Likert scale based on the answer to the essential question, meaning they will line up from "not at all" to "the most severe." Tomorrow, groups will present their conclusions.	__X__ Whole class ______ Small group ______ Pairs ______ Individual	Five minutes

Step 2: Collect the Data From an Assessment

After the lesson launch, the teacher creates a clear picture of what the end learning will be and establishes a rubric to accurately score performance, after which academic modeling and rehearsing begin. We regularly engage in conversations with teachers who are concerned with the overabundance of testing; duplications of various assessment tools that lead to both teacher and student fatigue; and difficult, time-consuming data-warehousing applications that many don't feel comfortable using. Data collection need not be fancy or burdensome. We feel teachers are best served when the tools they use collect evidence of student understanding and afford a quick turnaround for immediate action.

Collection of data comes from the specific tasks that teachers have drawn from the standards in step 1 (figure 4.6, pages 74–75). A CFU aligned to discrete learning targets will determine if students get it or not. The following outline describes what the data-collection process might look like in the global trade example and includes a variety of assessment types.

- For the preassessment, students individually create a KWL graphic organizer related to the topic of study to find out what they know, want to know, and have learned. In response to the preassessment, the teacher sorts the responses to begin to organize possible expert groups for specific research and fact-finding on the topic. This method is done quickly and easily by looking for similar topics of interest. After sorting the categories, the teacher notes the following findings.
    - Five students are interested in trade routes, specific rules of the sea, and types of seacraft.
    - Sixteen students have determined the following topics they would like to know more about in expert groups: people, transportation, imported and exported natural resources, finance, and miscellaneous. The assignment will require these students to access accurate information using text, interviews, and the Internet.
- After the teacher has conducted a whole-group lesson to build background for the entire class, there are five students who know absolutely nothing about the topic. The teacher engages in direct instruction followed by an exit card to determine if they now get it. Students use a notecatcher (see figure 4.9) so the teacher can check in during direct instruction, individual research time, or as an exit slip. They are asked to use cues to show how they now feel about the learning, as follows.

- **Thumbs-up:** These are the things I know and understand.
- **Lightbulb:** This was a new discovery for me.
- **Question mark:** Here is what I still don't understand.

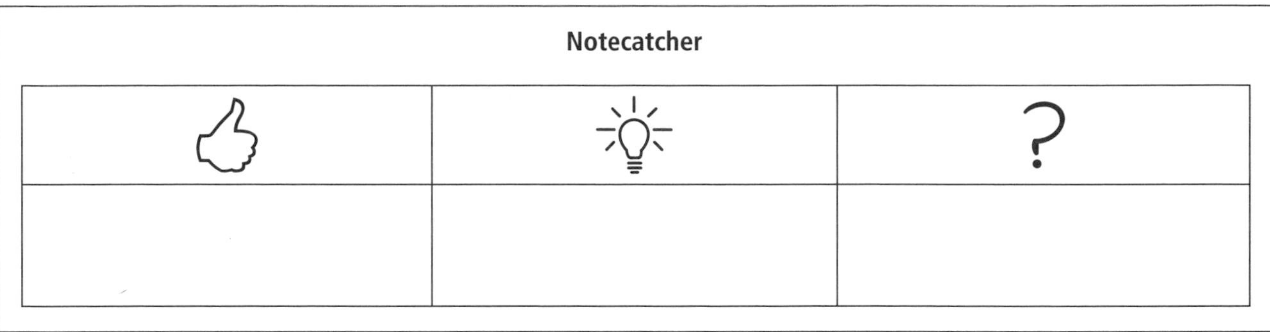

Figure 4.9: Notecatcher.

Visit ***go.SolutionTree.com/instruction*** *for a free reproducible version of this figure.*

The formative check-in consists of three additional assessment tasks.

- **Assessment task 1:** Students will use the chapter definitions from the unit to identify, match, and apply the vocabulary in sentences to a real-world application.
- **Assessment task 2:** Students will receive true and false statements that require them to use their unit vocabulary words, text, and maps to answer the questions. Note that the teacher is only asking five questions to collect evidence of student knowledge. A CFU should be short, concise, and focused on only one or two learning targets. Figure 4.10 provides a text-evidence template for recording students' conceptions on various statements. Students may track their own learning in the template, and the teacher may choose to use a student observation checklist for practices of accountability and student self-assessment.
- **Assessment task 3:** From the completed notecatchers (figure 4.9), expert groups will develop a fact-and-question center based on the five expert groups. All students will choose one of the five experts to join based on their interest. The teacher helps create tasks to cover the social studies material and provide opportunities to venture beyond the textbook to use multiple resources.

Statement	True	False	How Do You Know?
1.			
2.			
3.			
4.			
5.			

Figure 4.10: Text-evidence template.

Visit ***go.SolutionTree.com/instruction*** *for a free reproducible version of this figure.*

As the unit unfolds, the teacher keeps a running record of student work by using a class chart. The teacher maintains fixed learning targets for all students, but students have a choice on how they do, show, and tell about their tasks. Figure 4.11 (page 80) provides a chart for teachers to keep track of students' progress and mastery of the learning targets. Teachers write students' initials or first names in the boxes when they have mastered the targets based on the various assessments.

	Target 1	Target 2	Target 3	Target 4	Target 5	Target 6	Target 7	Target 8
Preassessment I								
Preassessment 2								
Assessment task 1								
Assessment task 2								
Quiz 1								
Assessment task 3								
Assessment task 4								
Assessment task 5								
Quiz 2								
Assessment task 6								
Assessment task 7								
Chapter test 1								

Figure 4.11: Class learning target recording sheet.

Visit ***go.SolutionTree.com/instruction*** *for a free reproducible version of this figure.*

Step 3: Interpret the Data

Once students have completed the assignment, the teacher scores them based on the criteria. Grade-level teams or individual teachers examine strong and weak work and meet with students to monitor, self-assess, and write further goals. The aim here is to gather rich data that informs where to go next instructionally. Many times, data can be collected but can be information poor. So many times, the student completes the product, the teacher records the grade, and they march to the next unit. However, we can't change our practice without reflecting on experiences. Ongoing reflection on assessment data is critical to raising the bar on performance. Table 4.4 is an example of initial data collection from the global trade assessments for a grade-level team. Teachers working alone would only fill in their own information, or list multiple classes' data if appropriate.

Table 4.4: Interpreting Data Chart—Grade-Level Team Example

Social Studies Summative Assessment Results					
Standard	**Teacher A**	**Teacher B**	**Teacher C**	**Teacher D**	**Learning Target Average**
Infer	87 percent	92 percent	96 percent	88 percent	91 percent
Cite text evidence	84 percent	90 percent	90 percent	75 percent	85 percent
Summarize	90 percent	86 percent	95 percent	82 percent	88 percent
Write an argument	85 percent	88 percent	90 percent	72 percent	84 percent
Classroom average	86 percent	89 percent	93 percent	79 percent	87 percent

Since teachers have deliberately invested time to teach a consistent curriculum and then write an assessment to match the instruction, the next logical conversation or teacher reflection process is to consider student proficiency after collecting grades. Whether you function as a singleton teacher or a collaborative team, next-step instruction focuses on the following six questions.

1. Where should the conversations begin after we have collected these data?
2. What determinations can we make from examining the learning target totals and the classroom totals?
3. Where are the collective learning target strengths?
4. Where are the collective learning target weaknesses?
5. What specific strategies have we each used that helped students understand better?
6. What specific strategies did students struggle to understand?

It is important to take another step to look at individual students' data, realizing that the data for the class as a whole did not provide the necessary information to provide feedback or plan next steps in instruction for individual students. Table 4.5 shows class data reported in percentages.

Table 4.5: Interpreting Data Chart—Class Example

	Infer	Cite Text Evidence	Summarize	Write an Argument	Student Learning Target Averages
Student 1	80	88	84	88	85
Student 2	92	66	88	75	80
Student 3	100	82	92	94	92
Student 4	66	70	72	68	69
Student 5	90	78	88	88	86
Student 6	82	80	94	90	87
Student 7	94	96	96	94	95
Student 8	100	90	98	96	96
Student 9	64	72	70	62	67
Student 10	84	78	72	70	76
Student 11	98	90	90	92	93
Student 12	70	76	78	74	75
Student 13	68	58	70	66	66
Student 14	94	94	92	96	94
Student 15	84	86	90	88	87
Learning Target Averages	84 percent	80 percent	85 percent	83 percent	83 percent

As teachers begin to consider their own classroom data, the greatest concentration should be on the following two questions:

- Which specific students need my greatest attention as we move ahead?
- Which specific students can I support through reinforcement and enrichment?

Examining the data further, a collaborative team will realize that it needs more specific information than a composite percentage to identify what its students know and understand in relation to the standards and learning targets. The team will also need students to take action based on the assessment information.

Step 4: Take Action

At this point, teachers ask students to look at their assessments and self-reflect on their personal learning for the unit by reviewing the learning goals, identifying accuracy of their work and reasons for their answers, and then ultimately writing a plan of future action to continue the learning. Teachers will include all priority standards in the student-reflection sheet since this includes the non-negotiable learning required. Figure 4.12 features a student reflection sheet for the global trade unit. Note that students have three opportunities to prove whether they know and understand each target.

Identifying My Strengths and Areas for Improvement

Global Trade Assessment

Name: ______________________________ Date: ______________

Learning Target	Sure	Unsure	Correct	Incorrect	Simple Mistake	More Study
1. Cite specific textual evidence to support analysis of primary and secondary sources.	X		X			
2. Cite specific textual evidence to support analysis of primary and secondary sources.	X		X			
3. Cite specific textual evidence to support analysis of primary and secondary sources.	X			X	X	
4. Determine central ideas or information in a primary or secondary source; provide an accurate summary.	X			X		X
5. Determine central ideas or information in a primary or secondary source; provide an accurate summary.		X		X		X
6. Determine central ideas or information in a primary or secondary source; provide an accurate summary.		X		X		X
7. Choose the meaning of words and phrases as they are used in a text.	X		X			
8. Choose the meaning of words and phrases as they are used in a text.	X		X			
9. Choose the meaning of words and phrases as they are used in a text.	X		X			

Sure: I know I got this right.
Unsure: I am not sure if I understand this.
Correct: I was correct in my thinking.
Incorrect: I was incorrect in my thinking.

Simple Mistake: After reviewing my work, I found I made a simple mistake that I have now corrected, and I understand now.
More study: I do not understand this question, and I need help.

Figure 4.12: Student self-reflection sheet.

Visit ***go.SolutionTree.com/instruction*** *for a free reproducible version of this figure.*

After self-reflecting, the student writes a specific action plan to continue his or her learning and growth (with or without the assistance of the teacher) and set future goals. A simple version of goal setting is the plan, do, check, and act process. Students answer the following questions.

- What is my *plan*?
- What will I *do*?
- How will I *check* to find the correct answer?
- What *action* will I take to improve my learning?

This helps students focus on where they are in their learning and what they will need to do for their next steps. Figure 4.13 provides a template for students to set goals based on this structure.

Plan, Do, Check, and Act	Specific Steps I Will Take	Date Completed
What is my plan?		
What will I do?		
How will I check?		
After checking, how will I act to improve my learning?		

Figure 4.13: Plan, do, check, and act goal-setting template.

Visit ***go.SolutionTree.com/instruction*** *for a free reproducible version of this figure.*

Step 5: Assess Summatively

We have shown how the various types of assessment—especially preassessment, checks for understanding, formative assessment, and student self-assessment—all work together throughout a unit to inform the teacher's next steps for instruction and to build student understanding not only of the content but of their own progress. This leads to the final step in the unit: summative assessment. Summative assessment can be a unit test, paper, demonstration, practical application project, or a choice of any and all of these. For the global trade unit, some students opted for writing an opinion piece addressing the essential questions in the unit. Some of the students in class chose an essay test for their summative assessment. Others opted to script and perform a debate on alliances, trade, and ecology. These students consulted one of our favorite websites (www.procon.org) to find data to defend their positions. We highly recommend the use of this wonderful website to provide data for research, generate interesting questions, and pique student interest.

As we've demonstrated throughout this chapter, assessment is much more than a number. In fact, we will be so bold as to say that reducing a high-quality project to a percentage simply does not do it justice. In the next section, we will demonstrate the value of such high-quality projects, providing three exemplars.

Exploring Project- and Performance-Based Learning

Project-based learning (PBL) is the hottest ticket in town when considering the importance of student engagement. PBL is an authentic way to launch, consolidate, and assess with purpose. While PBL is not exclusively dedicated to assessment, we have embedded PBL in this chapter on assessment because it is very possibly the most authentic type of assessment students can perform. If we begin with the end in mind, students will be ultimately assessed on what they know after their project is completed.

The assessments we have described in this chapter are largely pencil-and-paper-based tools that quantify learning; however, choosing a hybrid of written summative assessments and project-based learning is a win-win combination. Rather than a paper-and-pencil test, in PBL, students are expected to do, show, or tell what they have learned throughout the project experience. PBL very simply is an inquiry-based teaching method that allows students to frame their extended investigation around a meaningful problem or compelling question to answer. It features a real-world context focused on standards-based content and skills and includes critical thinking, self-management, and collaboration. When students use personal concerns and interests to invest in authentic tasks, this is the essence of PBL. Due to sharing and exposure of these projects, students invest more of their time in creating a project worthy of multiple eyes that see the final products.

The following scenarios are three outstanding examples of rigorous, meaningful PBL processes in which students share their work, and they are being implemented in classrooms of teachers we know personally.

Kids Care Company: Elementary PBL

Every teacher wishes to have a classroom full of students who not only can perform well academically but care for others, as well. Such is the case in the classroom of Judy Korsmo at Ben Franklin Elementary School in Grand Forks, North Dakota. Korsmo originated the Kids Care Company and has been successfully implementing it since 1982. She developed a way her fourth-grade students could integrate social studies, language arts, and civic responsibility, as well as model what it means to be a caring person in a hurting world.

Her first project with the Kids Care Company was having her students make greeting cards and sell them to parents, community members, and friends, with the proceeds going to designated charities that included the Humane Society, an orphanage in Haiti, missions in Mexico, local children in need, and a program called Ethiopia Reads.

Since greeting cards became more difficult to create, maintain, and sell, Korsmo invited her fourth-grade colleagues and their students to join the project and designate thirty minutes a day for eight to ten days in late fall to make gift tags and gift bags to raise awareness on behalf of needy causes in the community and abroad. Collectively, they typically raise $600–$1,000 during a two-week time period around Christmas. Additionally, students learn about company standards of excellence and how to market a strong product. Each student drafts ideas for product messaging; edits, revises, and creates them; targets a market (with parents, grandparents, neighbors, and so on) with a face-to-face sales opportunity; fills order forms; and delivers the product. After the students have tallied all orders, they collect and count the money, making certain their Kids Care Company books are balanced. They work collaboratively to help each other make a quality product and will often interview each other and include direct quotes from their classmates about the virtues of the Kids Care Company, which they include in a promotional letter they write to the public when soliciting orders. One student reflected that this was one of the best projects he had done because it made him feel so good inside. We cannot diminish project-based curricula like this to a percentage marked in a gradebook. It's a life lesson these students will never forget. As a gift to the students for a job well done, Korsmo gives the students a piece of fine chocolate for them to savor, much like these nine- and ten-year-olds will savor for a lifetime the memories of the impact they have made.

Kiva Microlending: Middle School PBL

William M. Ferriter, sixth-grade teacher in South Carolina and author and presenter, has found multiple ways to empower students through what he calls *purpose-driven curriculum*. The idea (as many of us can attest) is that students are naturally motivated to change the world, so create a curriculum that gives them an opportunity to do so, and they will run with it. With an integrated focus on social studies and language arts, the students engage in persuasive writing and evaluation. They research the demographics, assets, and liabilities of underdeveloped, developing, and fully developed countries and become motivated to change the financial scenario for many through a nonprofit microlending agency called Kiva. *Microlending* is a process by which small loans are made at low interest rates to entrepreneurs in need, often in developing nations.

Ferriter uses Kiva as a vehicle to empower his students through this life-changing venture that assists men, women, and children from underdeveloped countries in starting and sustaining businesses that provide a living for numerous families in need. Indeed, the program has provided hope for thousands of people who now have a future because students, clubs, and numerous individuals around the globe have assisted them as lending partners and changed their lives. Now that's curriculum in action! And it starts with a mere $25 commitment.

Students begin to explore the possibilities of assisting innovative, aspiring businesspeople who have marketable products but extremely low capital to get their ideas off the ground. Students research the cost of living, natural resources, education, and so on in multiple places on the world map. Rather than pick this platform out of thin air simply because it was a cool idea, Ferriter saw it was a perfect fit for the sixth-grade curriculum with a value-added, real-world application. The altruistic focus of this lending program gives purpose and has lifelong implications as students find meaning in the curriculum.

In order to earn funds to begin their lending process, students use their research to create action-oriented persuasive writing to share with businesses to plead their case and win support. They hold fundraisers, involve the PTA, and launch projects and raffles with the student council to raise both awareness and a financial foundation for the Kiva project. Do Something Funny for Money Day has been a huge success for the charity and builds buy-in across the school and community. As the momentum heightens for the project launch, students feel the power of their voices. In addition to raising funds, students read, understand, and employ appropriate fundraising rules and protocols, which make this a lasting experience that gives rise to thinking about their futures as entrepreneurs.

Projects such as this are certainly engaging; students see the impact of their humanitarianism and empowered decision making. The project began with a mere $200 that funded eight loans of $25 each. After many years now in the program, the several generations of sixth graders have continued to loan three to four times a week, and to date, they have issued more than four thousand loans in seventy-one countries with a cash reserve of $21,000 to continue to give so others can live more prosperously. Now that's exponential giving, and the only requirements to get started are teams of civically minded students willing to work collaboratively and a computer to communicate and manage their gifts of compassion across the globe. We invite readers to check out www.kiva.org for more details on how they can continue this legacy of giving in their own schools or organizations.

Simulated Workplace: High School PBL

Rigorous, student-centered engagement leads to high levels of student success, lowers school dropout rates, and promotes a lifelong love of learning. To support these outcomes, the West Virginia Department of Education began an exciting and innovative initiative called Simulated Workplace (SW), which empowers students to be accountable and prepared for the world of work.

Simulated Workplace transforms classrooms into simulated future workplaces directly tied to student interests and career goals. For example, a welding class transforms into a fabrication company; a hospitality and tourism class transforms into an event-planning company; a business class, depending on the area of concentration, transforms into a human resources firm, an accounting firm, or a marketing company; an English class may simulate a publishing company. This engages students in rigorous, exciting, and fun learning. Though the program takes place in a career technical education setting, the fact is that this concept works in any classroom, whatever the content. When students experience firsthand how learning directly relates to their future, the buy-in is immediate, fun, and meaningful.

West Virginia Department of Education personnel worked directly with state business leaders to design the program in response to the need of businesses and industries for public schools to graduate students who are career ready with marketable skills for the workplace, including: completing employment applications and being prepared for job interviews; arriving at work promptly; providing the employer with quality and a full day's work; understanding workplace safety; being drug free; understanding how companies operate and the importance of quality improvement; and understanding the roles of employees within a company and how employees' actions impact a company's bottom line.

In this program, the normal classroom setting becomes an industry-inspired workplace staged for business as the students form a company, transform into employees, and explore varied positions and roles within the company. Students even participate in business and industry yearly onsite evaluations. Simulated Workplace uses a portfolio system for students to document learning and skills, credentials earned, projects completed, and other pertinent evidence that tells their personal stories of career and college readiness. Simulated Workplace is not a curriculum but a learning environment shift, and teachers can implement it in any traditional classroom.

One example of a project from this program that illustrates the impact and real-world application of this PBL is Big Hearts Give Tiny Homes, which provided immediate response to devastating flooding in June 2016 that affected White Sulphur Springs and Greenbriar, West Virginia. Students in Simulated Workplaces participating in Big Hearts Give Tiny Homes constructed tiny houses, and by Christmas of the same year they delivered them to needy families who had lost their homes—complete with a Christmas tree and gifts. In December 2016, the students and faculty of the Simulated Workplaces involved in this project were recognized for their efforts by the West Virginia Department of Education, West Virginia governor Earl Ray Tomblin, and West Virginia senator Joe Manchin (West Virginia, 2016). Due to the success involved in launching this project, Simulated Workplace has now received national recognition and will be undertaking further humanitarian projects for Habitat for Humanity. It is a fantastic program worthy of replicating nationwide. The student investment is off the charts. To learn more about Simulated Workplace, visit www.simulatedworkplace.com and see West Virginia Department of Education (n.d.).

For more opportunities to create dynamic and authentic project-based learning lessons, we recommend exploring the Global Digital Citizen Foundation on the web (http://globaldigitalcitizen.org; also see Global Digital Citizen Foundation, n.d.). It is an outstanding resource for orchestrating inquiry-based learning in an organized and manageable fashion.

Conclusion

Assessment is a topic largely debated and largely misunderstood today. It has many complex aspects, and when done well serves as a means to promote learning, not shut learning down, as unfortunately so often happens. The best assessment continues learning in the form of specific feedback and information on which students will be able to take action. Too often, assessment is another name for getting the necessary scores and percentages recorded in gradebooks in order to report a grade. However, assessment is about learning and is so much more than a number.

Now that we have explored assessment design, we include a few tips for teachers to keep in mind as they create and implement their own assessments.

- Only teach what is important enough to assess. Avoid distraction with tasks that do nothing more than fill a space but do not contribute to academic integrity.
- Limit the amount of skills assessed at one time to ensure quality and a laser focus on the learning.

- Remember the objective of doing fewer things better and more deeply. Know the overarching big ideas, engage students in tasks that relate to their lives, and then move over and let them dig in.
- Think of the relationship to students in the learning process as analogous to that of a GPS to a driver. The GPS is programmed with many destinations (standards) but the driver needs to take the wheel to get there (engagement and ownership).

We must teach students to invest in themselves rather than simply fill in the blanks or find others to do it for them. Behind each set of data, there is a student. And behind each student is a mind engineered and empowered to think, represent, explore, explain, and innovate. Scores should act as a launching pad for continued ways to learn. When we release students to engage in meaningful tasks, rather than rigidly collecting numbers to quantify their learning, we have truly transitioned from simply teaching for the purpose of grading to placing a laser focus on students' learning.

The Takeaways

To fully assess students and to promote ongoing learning, consider the following points.

- Align *all* assessments to the unit's standards, KUDs, and learning targets.
- Use all forms of assessment: preassessment, checks for understanding, formative assessment, student self-assessment, and summative assessment.
- Use feedback more often than grades in order to continue the learning process for students.
- Use a comprehensive system to gather data, inform students, and adjust teaching as you move through the unit to the culminating event: summative assessment.
- Project- and performance-based learning is a dynamic way for students to actively explore real-world challenges in ways they do not often see in the classroom and simultaneously make a difference through their actions.

Glossary of Assessment Terms

assessment. Systematic collection, review, and use of information undertaken for the purpose of improving student learning (Palomba & Banta, 1999).

benchmarking. Measurement of group performance against an established standard administered at a specific point along the path toward accomplishing the standard.

criterion-referenced assessment. Tests created to measure student understanding against a specific set of concisely written criteria that tells whether a student is proficient at his or her grade level.

end-of-course classroom assessment. An ongoing collection of what students have learned and designed to examine a course to provide improvement.

embedded assessment. An authentic means of collecting evidence of student learning that is a natural part of the teaching and learning cycle; can be both formative and summative in nature.

direct assessment. A means of collecting evidence of student learning through performance, using criteria to determine value aligned to the standards.

evaluation. The use of assessment findings (evidence or data) to judge program effectiveness; used as a basis for making decisions about program changes or improvement (Allen, Noel, Rienzi, & McMillin, 2002).

formative assessment. The gathering of information about student learning during the progression of a course or program, usually repeatedly, to improve the learning of those students (Leskes, 2002).

indirect assessment. The gathering of information that tells how students feel about learning through surveys, questionnaires, interviews, focus groups, and reflective essays.

learning outcomes. Statements describing specific student behaviors that show knowledge, skills, abilities, or attitudes (Allen, Noel, Rienzi, & McMillin, 2002).

norm-referenced assessment. An assessment that compares and ranks student, school, district, or state performance in relation to a larger *norm group*.

performance criteria. Standards that evaluate student performance and provide students with expectations in order to hit their learning targets.

portfolio. An organized collection of student work that provides direct evidence of a student's efforts and progress over time. It can include numerous student-selected artifacts that demonstrate knowledge and understanding, such as assignments, projects, multimedia, reflections, and so on.

qualitative assessment. Data that is collected through observation, surveys, case studies, and interviews and that is used in depth to find how individuals feel, think, and exist but is never numerically measured.

quantitative assessment. Data collected through statistical comparisons and facts, composed of objective information that can be easily measured (for example, the baby weighs five pounds, seven ounces).

rubric. Set of criteria that define acceptable and unacceptable performance descriptors and assign values to each level.

standards. Levels of tasks students are expected to do, show, and tell about their knowledge and skills.

summative assessment. Collection of concrete information at the end of a learning cycle (usually reported by grades, percentages, or rubrics), which determines levels of proficiency and what to do next instructionally.

References

Allen, M., Noel, R. C., Rienzi, B. M., & McMillin, D. J. (2002). *Outcomes assessment handbook*. Long Beach: California State University, Institute for Teaching and Learning.

Leskes, A. (2002). Beyond confusion: An assessment glossary. *Peer Review, 4*(2/3). Accessed at www.aacu.org/publications-research/periodicals/beyond-confusion-assessment-glossary on March 7, 2017.

Palomba, C. A., & Banta, T. W. (1999). *Assessment essentials: Planning, implementing, and improving assessment in higher education*. San Francisco: Jossey-Bass.

Twenty-Five Terrific Checks for Understanding

Checks for understanding are typically gauges of student understanding and are ungraded and quick. Each of the following strategies can be adjusted to be used as a formative assessment, as well. This will be determined by the grade level, reading level or content complexity, and the intensity of the question prompt. Teachers should first model each CFU or formative assessment for students and release students to complete the tasks on their own when they are familiar with the structure.

1. **Author Sound Off:** Students respond by describing what they think the author's perspective is on a certain topic, citing evidence for their conclusion. This can be adapted for a mathematics or science text as well by having students respond to strategies, habits of mind, or reasoning that the author demonstrates.
2. **What? So What? Now What? Response:** Teachers give students a template to record their thinking on a topic. The What includes only facts. The So What includes the implications of the facts (cause and effect). The Now What is a prediction of future action or a solution to a problem. This is similar to and can be adapted from the template in figure 6.14 (page 127) that we provide for professional collaborative teams.
3. **Weighing In:** Use a two-column notes chart (see figure 3.8, page 48) to list opinions about the content in the left column and a justification for student thinking in the right column. The left column can also be used to record notes, definitions, or any other lesson content, and the right side can be used to record student interpretation, musings, and questions regarding the content.
4. **Mighty Mind Map:** With the use of web tools that create flow charts or diagrams, students create a mind map connected to a teacher prompt or content of their choice. The tool provides students and teachers with a link to access students' thinking processes. Mind map sites could include http://bubbl.us and http://popplet.com.
5. **Dynamite Dialogue:** The teacher or students extract a power-packed passage and express what it means to them. This same strategy can be used for unpacking multistep, open-ended mathematics and science problems as well.
6. **Rationale Race:** This CFU can be done individually or in pairs, triads, or teams. Have students identify at least five of the most interesting, challenging, or controversial ideas found in the content and include a short (one hundred words or fewer) rationale for their thinking. To heighten participation and interest, students, pairs, or groups race to justify their thinking. A judge is assigned to each group to determine which rationale is most convincing, and a point is awarded to the winner. Student engagement is high with this activity.
7. **Extra, Extra! Read All About It!:** Students create an advertisement, editorial, or short news story supported with visuals and powerful text related to the content. For a shorter version, have students create headlines or bumper stickers to summarize the main points of any lesson.
8. **Sensing With Six:** Have students choose six words related to the senses to describe a character, a story, or selected content and justify their choices.
9. **Amazing Analogy:** Students explain their thinking by using a personal analogy.
10. **Poetic Justice:** Students select eight to ten words from a text and create a poem highlighting the chosen words. Students summarize their understanding of the highlighted words. The poem could be adapted to a process or problem-solving strategy in other content areas.
11. **Teacher Tune-Up:** The teacher provides a checklist of criteria for students to make tune-up improvements to their written response and make their thinking tighter. Written responses in mathematics would include explanations and justifications of strategies, procedures, and answers.

page 1 of 2

12. **Polar Opposites:** Students choose an idea or theory that the author has proposed, and then take opposition to it.
13. **Give It Definition:** Students select a word, phrase, or passage and attach a personal meaning and example to it.
14. **Clear or Muddy Mind:** Students rate their understanding of the assigned content from clear to muddy and identify why there is clarity or confusion.
15. **Sentence Stems:** Students fill in the following sentence stem regarding the lesson.
    I am frustrated (or *confused*, *excited*, *perplexed*, *intrigued*) by ________________ because ____.
16. **Gonna Take You Higher:** Students write seven higher-order thinking questions related to the assigned reading or problem-solving task and exchange their questions with a classmate. They then choose two of the questions they receive to respond to. This requires modeling by the teacher first, but the student investment factor is critical here.
17. **Traffic-Light Response:** The teacher gives the students a prompt, and they respond by holding up a green card when they understand, a yellow card when they are uncertain, or a red card when they do not understand the concept or skill.
18. **Bold Bullets:** Students represent understanding by outlining the major points of an assigned reading by bulleting words or phrases that resonate. Bullets can also be used to have students design or elicit a step-by-step process or as reasoning prompts for a specific mathematics or science topic.
19. **Sticky Points:** Students use sticky notes to annotate a text by identifying notable words, phrases, or passages that they find interesting or confusing in any subject area.
20. **Top 10:** Using humor, students make a list of ten of the most important takeaways from an assignment.
21. **Conference Corner:** Students are paired and select a spot of their choice in the classroom to confer with one another about a teacher-created or student-created question.
22. **Sketch It!:** Have students illustrate new knowledge through visual representation.
23. **Drama:** Choose a complex narrative and have students act out a critical scene from it. This can be adapted to playing charades to have the class guess key vocabulary in any content area, as well.
24. **Masterful Minute:** Students describe the most meaningful component of the lesson in one minute or less.
25. **TED Talks:** Introduce students to a number of TED Talk experiences to provide a model for a successful classroom TED Talk.

CHAPTER 5

ADAPTING INSTRUCTION THROUGH DIFFERENTIATION

A new school year has begun at South Middle School, and the sixth-grade rosters reflect an average of twenty-six students per class. Teachers have created an inviting atmosphere that includes desks arranged in student learning groups of four, decorative bulletin boards, a computer center, a reading corner dressed with both old and new titles for the adolescent reader, and a writer's conferencing corner equipped with all the writing and editing tools the young writer needs. They have placed new texts on each desk, ready for the eager learners to begin their march through the content. The teachers have been feverishly digging into lesson plans that not only ignite the interest of learners as the new year begins but become a catalyst for laying the foundation for classroom policies, procedures, and protocols for the rest of the year.

During the first few weeks, teachers conduct student preassessments to determine academic, social, and emotional strengths and weaknesses. Though they effectively organize and execute all plans, programs, and protocols, it becomes clear that there are immense learning gaps. Some students need placid, unruffled structure, while others need more socialization and group interplay. Some build a case in defense of their answers (whether correct or incorrect), and others seek concrete, analytic problem solving with little wiggle room for negotiation. A handful of students are quick to solve equations while others exhibit lengthy, verbal deliberation. Some students are distant, developmentally delayed, nonverbal, or socially awkward. Others find self-heightened curiosity as they voluntarily share new knowledge with one another. Some students behave inappropriately or are disengaged from the learning. It isn't necessarily that these students don't want to learn. Conversely, they act out because they don't know *how* to learn and don't want to bring attention to their academic inadequacies.

In addition to all the other moving parts, several migrant families have moved to the district, and a huge language barrier exists for the students who have limited English abilities. Autistic students are finding entirely too much stimulation and those with attention deficits are zinging off the wall. Teachers' plates are full to overflowing as they wonder how these circumstances will impact the essential content they need to teach.

Our students look, act, and perform in many different ways, with varying degrees of success and proficiency. The key for teachers is to work with the talents students have and develop attitudes and behaviors that lead to success. The best, well-made instructional plans can go awry because one size does not fit all. This is not to say that some students cannot learn or be successful but rather that the ways in which students learn and their needs for reaching success are diverse. As Theodore R. Sizer (2004) states, "That students differ may be inconvenient, but it is inescapable. Adapting to that diversity is the inevitable price of productivity, high standards, and fairness to the students" (p. 194).

In chapter 4, we shared multiple ways students can be assessed, but behind every piece of data is a face that represents the students we serve. The real heavy lifting takes place when we use data collection to move us to instructional action. This is the essence of adaptive teaching. Fisher and Frey (2015) note, "This may be as simple as finding conceptual errors or as complex as redesigning lessons that fail to meet the intended learning goals" (p. 11). Adapting responsively to student needs requires us to know and understand how to differentiate or discern where to go next on the path to proficiency for each and every student.

In this chapter, we examine how to adapt to student needs by differentiating instruction. There are obviously numerous, information-rich, complete books on differentiated instruction written in greater depth than we provide in this chapter. We intend this chapter to be for teachers seeking a general overview. We recommend that teachers start this process by doing a few things well and then adding more to their toolboxes each year. The main areas in which teachers can build their toolboxes, which we'll focus on in this chapter, are (1) creating responsive classrooms, (2) identifying basis and areas for differentiation, and (3) getting started with differentiation.

Creating Responsive Classrooms

Would it stand to reason that if students don't understand through the ways we currently teach, we need to teach them in the way they most effectively learn? That is the essence of differentiation. Scenarios similar to that of South Middle School play out in nearly every classroom in America, and the need for responsive teaching (responding to differing student needs) is enormous. Highly effective teachers in these classrooms resort to best practices steeped in *differentiated instruction*. Differentiated instruction is a method of using varying instructional strategies and lesson delivery to reach students responsively. Ongoing, short-cycle formative assessment, performed typically within twenty-four to forty-eight hours, is an essential ingredient of this method and should be accompanied by descriptive, explicit, in-the-moment (immediate) feedback directly aligned to the end learning outcomes. To ensure a strong foundational understanding of responsive classrooms, in the following two sections, we'll examine the difference between traditional and differentiated classrooms and examine the components of differentiated, responsive classrooms.

Traditional Versus Differentiated Classrooms

How is differentiated, responsive instruction different than a traditional "stand and deliver" classroom model? Figure 5.1 depicts the content-coverage model delivered in a whole-class setting for the purpose of sorting and selecting—the ranking of students from highest to lowest academic performance. This model reflects a teaching philosophy of "I teach; you learn."

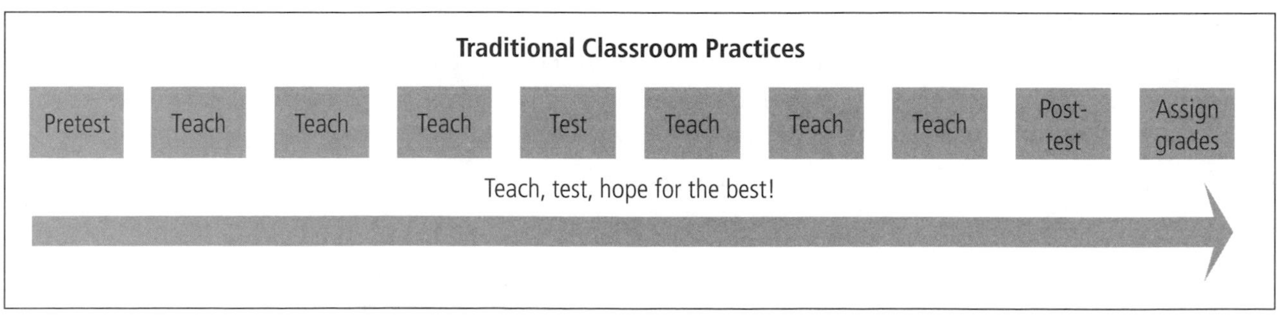

Figure 5.1: Content-coverage model.

The philosophy in this classroom is that the teacher's job is to tell and show students everything they need to know. If students don't get it, they can come in before or after school for extra help, but the teacher has to keep going or he or she will never finish teaching the required content. Content is king in this classroom, but learning is not always ensured.

PLC literature describes how the focus should be on *learning* (DuFour et al., 2016). To truly respond to the *learner*, we must restructure the instructional model as shown in figure 5.2. Note the placement of the star emphasizes that preassessment and analysis of student work have been done prior to differentiation. In contrast, the traditional model continues the content-coverage march without pausing to reflect on learning before more content is introduced.

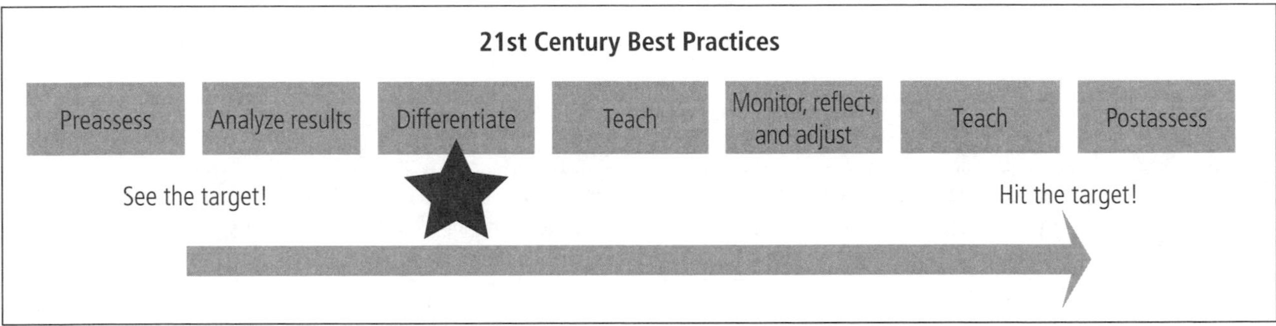

Figure 5.2: Student-centered, differentiated model.

The second model ensures that *all* learners have the opportunity to experience appropriate instruction based on assessment and analysis of the results. It provides a basis for differentiating for the diverse student population before instruction begins. The game changer is what happens in the formative checks for understanding when progress monitoring, student reflection, and partnering between the teacher and student take place to plan steps toward the end goal. In a student-centered classroom, learning is the focus and structure must respond accordingly. Differentiation accommodates this, but differentiation requires time for planning and execution. The process of analysis, differentiation, and teaching appears only once in the illustration in figure 5.2, but these items do not occur only once during a unit of instruction. The cycle of using a formative assessment to analyze learning, differentiate as needed, and then teach happens frequently throughout the unit. When the summative assessment arrives, all students have had many academic rehearsals in order to succeed on the assessment. This cycle compounds as the end of the school year approaches and high-stakes tests are in sight.

Seasoned educators know their content and aggressively plan to scaffold learning from simple to complex tasks in order to bridge the vast educational divide in their classrooms. Figure 5.3 examines the teaching approaches in traditional and differentiated classrooms and asks teachers to reflect and place a checkmark in the box that most resembles their style in the classroom.

Most Like Me	Teacher's Philosophical Statements in a Traditional Classroom	Teacher's Philosophical Statements in a Differentiated Classroom	Most Like Me
	"Covering the content is my first priority, and I call the shots instructionally."	"Since learning is the focus of my classroom, teaching is contingent on student needs and fidelity to a guaranteed and viable curriculum."	
	"Learning goals are the same for all students."	"Learning goals may be adjusted based on the needs of the students, but fidelity to the grade-level standards is maintained for all students."	

Figure 5.3: Traditional versus differentiated teacher conversations.

continued →

Most Like Me	Teacher's Philosophical Statements in a Traditional Classroom	Teacher's Philosophical Statements in a Differentiated Classroom	Most Like Me
	"We will emphasize mastery of content and skills."	"We will master content and skills through the lens of 21st century critical-thinking and problem-solving skills with a focus on real-world application."	
	"The textbook will be the foundation for our information."	"The world is our classroom, and students use multiple resources for learning. However, we follow content standards to ensure critical knowledge at grade level and beyond."	
	"I find whole-classroom instruction to be most beneficial and manageable for me."	"I make the content focus clear to my students and use multiple instructional formats to get at the learning through whole-class instruction and small groups, one-on-one instruction, and so on, based on student needs."	
	"Students are grouped homogeneously. It's more manageable to teach that way."	"Since learning is the constant, the structure of my room changes both heterogeneously and homogeneously, as needed."	
	"I teach at a constant pace in order to cover the needed curriculum by year's end."	"The pace of teaching is contingent on student need. Sometimes we need to move faster or slower but will catch the calendar up as we go."	
	"My students can expect the same type of instruction daily."	"Because of the multiple ways my students hear and process information, I vary my approach to include direct, explicit instruction; role playing; individual learning contracts; lecture; computer quests; and so on."	
	"I expect all students to complete all assigned work."	"I expect all students to complete the assigned work. However, I will compact, accelerate, eliminate, or adjust work based on preassessment, observation, and student feedback."	
	"All students are expected to complete the same assigned work."	"I design a variety of tasks for students to complete based on how my students learn. Some tasks may be teacher directed while others may include student choice."	
	"When students are having difficulty, I use whole-classroom instruction to reteach. "	"When students encounter difficulty and I need to reteach a lesson, I first determine whether the whole class needs to be retaught or if a small-group pull-out will suffice. I hold students accountable for the intended learning goals, but I try additional methods to get to the learning in new ways."	
	"I provide opportunities for students to be academically enriched by giving more content with deeper thinking required."	"I tier lessons to provide opportunities for all students on every stage of the learning continuum from struggling to advanced. I ensure that all students have the opportunity to complete tasks at all DOK levels and all stages of Bloom's taxonomy."	
	"My philosophy is 'I teach, you learn.'"	"My philosophy is that I will do whatever it takes for my students to learn."	

Visit ***go.SolutionTree.com/instruction*** *for a free reproducible version of this figure.*

As figure 5.3 (page 95) illustrates, the mindset of a teacher who differentiates is significantly different from those in traditionally modeled classrooms where the focus is covering material for students to memorize and regurgitate, grading them based on how much information they can recall on a test, and regarding the overall grade as the essence of learning. This traditional model has little to do with learning and functioning in the real world. On the contrary, what we know about 21st century learning is that reflection and specific, explicit feedback is necessary to engage the learner in the content. As they reflect honestly, teachers who find they identify with statements in the left-hand column can use this opportunity to challenge their mindset and set goals for growth.

Components of Differentiated, Responsive Classrooms

As we have illustrated, differentiated classrooms operate with a different philosophy than the traditional classroom. Implementing this philosophy and creating a student-centered, responsive classroom result in many value-added components. Note also the careful planning required to ensure the conditions that allow these components to flourish.

First, students use all their senses to learn. In a responsive classroom, teachers use auditory, visual, and kinesthetic supports frequently and provide variety. Some of the tools teachers will see in a classroom responsive to student learning preferences include *picture cards* that correspond to difficult vocabulary, creating meaning in the mind; *graphic organizers* that address key skills, leading to keener comprehension; *manipulatives* so students experience meaning with their hands; and of course, *modified seatwork and assessments* so students attend to the same skills as the rest of the classroom but work within their academic zone.

Differentiated-instruction classrooms also help develop multiple parts of the brain. Classrooms that focus on the body-and-mind connection employ cross-training techniques. Well-trained athletes work on all muscle groups in the body in order to be fully warmed up for practice or ready for rigorous competition. A runner needs to do more than stretch only his or her legs. The arms, torso, shoulders, and more need to be conditioned as well to perform optimally. Likewise, strong teachers cross-train students by using multiple approaches to develop many parts of their brains.

Choice is a regular guest in a differentiated-instruction classroom. Can you imagine eating tuna casserole for every meal because your mother mandated it? Tiring, correct? Why would this be any different for students who receive the same instruction, day after day, prepared and delivered in exactly the same way? Variety and choice are vital. The key to remember here is that teachers always hold students accountable for reaching the learning target, but they provide a scaffold, or learning progression, that builds to the end goal. Figure 5.4 gives one example of a structure balancing teacher-assigned tasks and student-choice tasks. In order for this template to take root with students, it is of utmost importance that the teacher models the process by assigning the Must Do learning tasks. Because the teacher is adapting learning to the needs of students, the Choose Two and Please Do items become invitations for students to show what they know in the way they best are able. These may be teacher designed, student designed, or a combination of the two. Where there is good modeling to understand the process, and then autonomy to continue the process, we have a win-win combination.

Must Do:

Students are required to do all tasks.

Task 1:

Task 2:

Task 3:

Task 4:

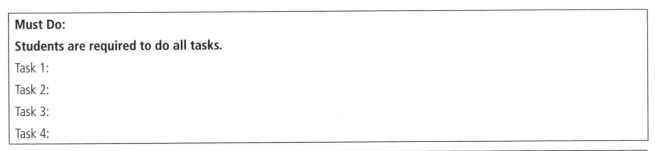

Figure 5.4: Balanced assignment structure.

continued →

Choose Two: **Students choose two of the choices.** Task 1: Task 2: Task 3: Task 4:
Please Do: **Students may choose one of the two optional choices.** Task 1: Task 2:

Visit ***go.SolutionTree.com/instruction*** *for a free reproducible version of this figure.*

In addition to making choices, in differentiated-instruction classrooms, students also self-monitor and prioritize. This encourages them to self-regulate and think independently. Establishing roots of responsibility and growing their independence fosters students' development of these essential skills for lifelong success.

Teachers in differentiated-instruction classrooms must ensure that a few conditions are in place from the beginning of the year or term in order to create and sustain their value.

- **Ensure that students understand up front that *fair* is not always *equal*:** Fair allows students the opportunity to do, show, and tell in the way they best can produce evidence of knowledge. When students understand this, it's possible to build a cooperative instead of competitive classroom.
- **Use flexible grouping:** Not all students, whether general education students or students with special needs, excel in the same ways. All students should work with all other students in a differentiated classroom. Grouping of students is constantly changing and is based on the specific task and manner in which it is differentiated. Students develop interdependence as they work both heterogeneously and homogeneously as necessary.
- **Set high expectations for *all* students:** Students rise to the expectations that we set—whether high or low.
- **Avoid labels and bias:** There is no room for student bias in a differentiated classroom. When we label students (and teachers, for that matter), we limit potential. Keep classroom goals attainable and support students with suitable resources while inviting numerous perspectives to emerge from a variety of learning styles.

To dig deeper, we want to put to rest some of the myths that surround the protocols, procedures, and processes of an effective differentiated classroom. Here's what we know does *not* exist in differentiated classrooms.

- Chaos and high levels of unproductive, ill-managed noise
- Much greater complexity and rigor for the brightest students and fewer or lower expectations of the struggling population
- Formulaic delivery of a specific set of "correct" strategies
- An individualized lesson plan for each student in the classroom

Ponder Box

Consider your current level of differentiation by responding to the following five questions.

1. Based on your responses to figure 5.3 (page 95), which instructional model do you most use: a traditional classroom or a differentiated classroom?
2. If you were to capture in a word or phrase each of the teaching styles (traditional and differentiated), what word or words would you use?
3. Since class building and team building are important in a differentiated classroom, how can you build community relatively quickly so students understand what *fair* and *equal* mean?
4. Is a rigorous academic curriculum important for all students in a differentiated-instruction classroom?
5. What user-friendly strategies do you currently use to address the diverse learning needs of your students?

Identifying Basis and Areas for Differentiation

Before teachers can design differentiation, they have to know their students. The very first step should be to assess students' readiness, interest, and learning profiles. These three types of student differences will provide the basis for the differentiation strategies teachers choose (Tomlinson, 2001).

1. **Readiness:** This term describes individual entry points into the learning, including prior knowledge, levels of independence, speed of learning, and so on. Very simply stated, when tasks are a close match for the student's developmental skills and understanding of the topic, the student is ready for optimal learning. Teachers collect the evidence of students' readiness through content preassessments, formative assessments, in-class observations, and more.
2. **Interest:** This term describes what will motivate students to learn. These tasks ignite curiosity and passion in the student to engage in the learning.
3. **Learning profile:** Learning profiles contain specific information a teacher keeps of each student that includes his or her learning styles, preferences, and so on. This includes the ways a student will best make sense of learning. The educator asks himself or herself, "What is the preferred manner of learning for this student?" Most teachers are familiar with learning modalities, which include students who prefer to learn and process information visually (visual), auditorily (auditory), or through more hands-on tasks (kinesthetic). Howard Gardner's (1983) theory of multiple intelligences can also help teachers in identifying students' learning styles and strengths. Briefly, Gardner identifies eight different abilities or *intelligences* that speak to people's predispositions to learn in a certain way: (1) musical-rhythmic, (2) visual-spatial, (3) verbal-linguistic, (4) logical-mathematical, (5) bodily-kinesthetic, (6) interpersonal, (7) intrapersonal, and (8) naturalistic. Educators may also be familiar with right-brain and left-brain dominance, and Robert Sternberg's (2005) triarchic theory of intelligence, which recognizes that some people make sense of new learning in one or a combination of the following ways: (1) analytical, (2) practical, and (3) creative, but there are many aspects to help determine learning profiles. Note, however, that these are not exhaustive lists.

There are inventories available that teachers can use to assess student interests and learning profiles. Perceptual surveys such as the example in figure 5.5 (page 100) are another way to gauge student interest.

Tap Dance

Check the activities you would like to "tap into" when your work has been done well.

_______ Draw or color

_______ Have extra computer time

_______ Have extended play time

_______ Be a study buddy in another classroom

_______ Be a messenger for the teacher

_______ Play with Legos, puzzles, construction blocks, or other toys and games

_______ Receive a "Good News Note" for home

_______ Get a special treat or snack

_______ Have extra time to be with friends

_______ Be head of the line

Figure 5.5: Survey for one aspect of student learning preferences.

Teachers can also establish learning profiles and use other inventories that provide insight into varied thinking processes to exercise and develop thinking. When teachers know their students' learning profiles, they can design strategies that strengthen learning in different parts of the brain, as well as match tasks best suited to students' preferred learning styles. Giving students surveys, such as the multiple intelligence survey in figure 5.6, for example, can also help students and teachers recognize areas of learning profiles.

	You Got It!	No Way!
1. My mind is wired for finding patterns.		
2. I like to generate ideas with others.		
3. I am made to move!		
4. I make wise choices.		
5. I enjoy working outside and growing plants.		
6. I like to sing and dance.		
7. I like being by myself.		
8. Word games get me "cranked!" I am good at these!		
9. I enjoy competition.		
10. I like to take care of animals.		
11. I could draw for hours!		
12. I like to write my own stories.		
13. I am interested in looking at pictures.		
14. I like cooperative work with others.		
15. I like to read maps.		
16. I enjoy reading books in my free time.		
17. I like tuning into the Weather Channel to follow weather patterns and trends.		

Figure 5.6: Multiple intelligence and learning styles inventory.

18. I like to touch, feel, and experience things through my senses.		
19. I enjoy poetry, rhythms, and rhymes.		
20. I enjoy being independent.		

Word Smart: 8, 12, 16

Mathematics Smart: 1, 15

Self Smart: 4, 7, 20

People Smart: 2, 14

Visually Smart: 11, 13

Nature Smart: 5, 10, 17

Music Smart: 6, 19

Body Smart: 3, 9, 18

Once teachers have identified readiness, interest, and learning profiles for every student, they will understand their students' needs well enough to proceed with differentiation by deciding what, specifically, to differentiate in their teaching.

According to Tomlinson (2001), there are four areas that teachers can differentiate: (1) content, (2) process, (3) product, and (4) learning environment. *Content* is what students will learn, *process* is what students will do in order to learn, *product* is what students will do to show they have learned, and the *learning environment* is the classroom structure and culture in which they learn. These four areas are part of every classroom, everywhere in the world, usually in the same ways for all students.

Content

When differentiating by content, align tasks to specific learning targets. Instruction is concept focused and principle driven. The teacher holds each student, regardless of his or her cognitive ability, accountable for the learning outcomes, but can adjust access to the information to ensure learning. Following are some examples of ways to differentiate the content.

- Use leveled texts and other varied resources.
- Offer a choice of graphic organizers.
- Allow a variety of ways for students to access the content, including reading, listening, and modeling and using text-based, computer-based, or lecture-based resources.

Process

We want to begin by making sure that all students understand the purpose for the learning activities, regardless of how we design activities for the different learning profiles. Not only can we differentiate the task, we can differentiate how we group the students, as well. Since not all students require the same amount of support from the teacher, he or she can flexibly design instruction to include working in pairs, small groups, or individually.

The most common way that teachers differentiate is to look at the specific tasks students will complete in order to learn the material. Examples of differentiating the process by modality (such as auditory, visual, and kinesthetic) include:

- Providing textbooks for visual and word learners
- Providing graphics, charts, and so on to amplify content
- Having students diagram or create visuals to help learn and remember
- Allowing auditory learners to listen to audiobooks

- Engaging students with whole-class and small-group discussions around provided guiding questions and talking points
- Encouraging students to explain and demonstrate learning through oral presentations
- Providing concrete materials or manipulatives to develop key ideas
- Incorporating movement into class structures
- Using games to learn and practice skills
- Giving kinesthetic learners the opportunity to complete an interactive assignment online

Product

Teachers will hold all students, regardless of their ability, accountable for the essential learning outcomes, but they have the opportunity to do, show, and tell their knowledge in different ways. The end goal is to collect evidence that students understand the learning outcome, not necessarily that they have used a specific format to show their understanding. Because of this, teachers can differentiate *how* students show their understanding through performance (do), product creation (show), or oral support of their learning (tell).

Following are some examples of ways to differentiate the product.

- Offer students a choice of assignments
- Plan varied working conditions students can choose from
- Design activities with stations that contain different tasks
- Provide a rubric or checklist of objectives, but allow students to choose whether to provide a written assessment, an oral assessment, or other project task
- Have a unit test with a section of required questions for a specified number of points and a section of optional questions to make up the balance of points

Learning Environment

A flexible classroom layout, incorporating various types of furniture and arrangements to support both individual and group work, is key. Psychologically speaking, teachers should use classroom management techniques that encourage a safe and supportive learning environment (Diamond & Hopson, 1999; Wong, Wong, Jondahl, & Ferguson, 2014). If differentiation is to flourish, the teacher must base the classroom culture on the idea that learning is the priority. Whatever a student needs to learn is what the student will get. Teachers should explicitly develop the idea that *fair* means getting what students need—and not sameness—within the learning community.

Following are some examples of ways to differentiate the learning environment.

- Break some students into small groups to discuss the assignment.
- Allow students to work individually if they prefer.
- If the school allows, let some students listen to music while working. Others may choose not to.
- Allow students to sit wherever they would like, including the floor, as long as they continue to work.

Getting Started With Differentiating

To begin to differentiate within the unit, deconstruct the unit's end-goal tasks (based on the KUD) into individual lesson tasks. Determine the required prerequisite skills for the learning targets, and consult the results of any preassessments or formative assessments that inform individual students' learning needs. Plan differentiated tasks to accomplish the lesson's objective.

Where does one begin with differentiation strategies? Simple is always better, and it is always best to begin with what makes most sense. Keep in mind there is not only one correct approach. Some teachers start differentiating using learning profiles or interest by providing choices. Others start through readiness. We advise teachers to start with what makes most sense for you and your students. Truthfully, the best way to start is to *start.* Our recommendation is to take time to plan thoughtfully in the beginning to ensure a successful experience. There is no "right" way. Begin where you are and then get better through experience. Do note, however, one way we should not differentiate is by quantity. Giving struggling students less of the work they do not understand and giving excelling students more of the same kind of work they already know how to do does not benefit anyone.

Table 5.1 lists strategies for differentiating content, process, and product based on readiness, interest, and learning profile. Keep the learning environment in mind for each of the strategies, and consider whether each would be best done in small groups, teams, as individuals, with teacher assistance, with or without music, as a whole class, or in smaller heterogeneous or homogeneous groupings.

Table 5.1: Strategies for Differentiation

	Readiness	**Interest**	**Learning Profile**
Content	Leveled texts Spelling lists based on unknown words Scaffolded notes Prerequisite review or extensions Curriculum compacting or acceleration for students with advanced prior knowledge	Book choice Choice of application problems Extension options Choice of graphic organizers	Varied access to content through reading, listening, or modeling Analytical, practical, and creative examples or explanations
Process	Tiered activities Station work based on formative assessment Small-group instruction	Jigsaw choices Interest centers Choice of assignments Choice of working conditions (music or no music; with partner or alone; sitting at desk, on the floor, or standing)	Tasks based on multiple intelligences Varied working conditions (small group, pairs, or individually)
Product	Personal agendas Tiered product tasks or rubrics Varied resources Varied check-in points	Choice of product formats Options within summative assessment (choose from a variety of tasks)	Written, oral, or modeled presentations Creative, analytical, or practical components of tests or products Varied do, show, or tell activities

Figure 5.7 (page 104) offers examples of teachers beginning their differentiated-isnstruction practices in their classrooms. The center column explains what observations the teacher makes that will influence differentiation.

<table>
<tr><th>Teacher</th><th>Teacher's Observations of Students</th><th>Beginning Differentiation</th></tr>
<tr><td>Mrs. Rex</td><td>Students read at many levels in her grade 3–4 multiage classroom.</td><td>Content by readiness</td></tr>
<tr><td colspan="3">Classroom Example:

Mrs. Rex asks her students to read appropriate texts based on reading Lexiles. She chooses books in the same genre that will complement each other and address the same learning, such as a common theme, a strong author's voice, and vivid vocabulary. Mrs. Rex is able to have whole-class discussions based on the lesson's KUDs and learning, with students contributing from their own specific reading. Sometimes, Mrs. Rex has students meet together based on the common reading to discuss questions. Other times, she mixes the reading groups to discuss common elements within their own readings, such as theme or voice.</td></tr>
<tr><th>Teacher</th><th>Teacher's Observations of Students</th><th>Beginning Differentiation</th></tr>
<tr><td>Mr. Huggins</td><td>Students in seventh-grade mathematics connect to learning through different processes and think and learn efficiently in very different ways.</td><td>Process by learning profile</td></tr>
<tr><td colspan="3">Classroom Example:

Mr. Huggins creates three different activities to find surface areas and volumes of compound shapes and asks students to choose one.

1. Students use empty cans and boxes, which they measure, fill with cubes to determine volume, and then "gift wrap" in order to determine surface area. Students relate the measurements, the physical results, and the formulas.
2. On graph paper, students draw nets to represent compound polyhedra, then use the nets to determine surface area and volume. They relate the graph paper results to the formula.
3. Pairs of students create a public service announcement skit to explain the difference between surface area and volume. They use examples with actual solids and drawings to explain the formulas.</td></tr>
<tr><th>Teacher</th><th>Teacher's Observations of Students</th><th>Beginning Differentiation</th></tr>
<tr><td>Mrs. Lewis</td><td>Students in freshman science didn't do their best work on chapter exams even though they seemed to truly understand content through formative assessments.</td><td>Product by interest</td></tr>
<tr><td colspan="3">Classroom Example:

After a botany unit, Mrs. Lewis requires all students to create a formal lab write-up but also gives students a choice of how to demonstrate their learning. They can choose one of the following three options.

1. Give a poster presentation.
2. Write a report followed by a short interview with Mrs. Lewis.
3. Record a PowerPoint presentation.</td></tr>
</table>

Figure 5.7: Differentiated classroom examples.

Beginning the work of planning differentiation can be a difficult process, but do not become discouraged. Instead, turn to and collaborate with colleagues to share ideas and tackle obstacles. We suggest grabbing a colleague as a fellow experimenter and giving differentiation a try while supporting one another. Come back together after trying one or two differentiated strategies in a three- to four-week period of time and discuss the following six questions.

1. What went well?
2. What was I, as the instructor, doing when learning occurred for the student or students?
3. What was difficult about using this differentiated-instruction strategy? Why?
4. In retrospect, what would I do differently as I organize and implement the strategy next time around?

5. What did I learn about the students and myself in the process?
6. Which strategy will we commit to in the next instructional cycle, and when will we meet to discuss our findings?

Ponder Box

Consider your own differentiation practices, and respond to the following four prompts.

1. When new learning occurs for both students and teachers alike, the quicker new knowledge can be applied, the greater the chances for sustainability. Decide on your next steps for differentiation. It will be best if you and a colleague can support each other through the experimentation.
2. What specific step or steps will you take to deepen and sustain new discoveries about differentiated instruction?
3. Which colleague might partner with you in the differentiated-instruction process to experiment with new strategies on behalf of student-centered learning? How will you make that happen?
4. What measurable goals will you construct to follow through with your plan of implementation?

Next, it's time to think about the specific students who will benefit from their commitment. For an upcoming lesson or unit, list specific students who will need a different method for learning or showing learning, ideas for what that might look like, and when in the unit it will happen. Figure 5.8 provides a template for planning.

Who?	What?	When?
Reflection:		

Figure 5.8: Differentiated-instruction planning template.

Visit ***go.SolutionTree.com/instruction*** *for a free reproducible version of this figure.*

Of course, once teachers have decided on their differentiated activities, they should be sure to enter them in in the Engagement Activities section of their lesson-plan template (figure 1.2, page 10). Refer to figure 3.12 (page 57) for an example of how a teacher might record this.

Differentiated instruction requires more work during lesson planning, especially in the beginning. Additionally, the learning curve can be steep, and some schools lack professional development resources. Unfortunately, differentiation has been viewed as a silver bullet in education. However, when educators have not invested time and resources to ensure proper implementation, it is easy to conclude that differentiation does not work. Implementing differentiated instruction is time consuming and is never done with perfection. It is messy and ongoing. There are many reasons for teachers to invest their time in differentiating instruction. From firsthand experience, we have witnessed the effectiveness of differentiated instruction for all students, and this goes beyond readiness levels alone. When students receive more options for learning the material, they take on more responsibility for their own learning. Students tend to be more engaged in learning, and there are fewer discipline problems in classrooms where teachers provide differentiated lessons (Tomlinson, Brimijoin, & Narvaez, 2008).

One example that embraces these approaches and is yielding these outcomes is personalized learning, which is enjoying growing popularity due to the support of Bill and Melinda Gates (Bill and Melinda Gates Foundation, n.d.). *Personalized learning* requires traditional districts to adjust the conditions of learning in their schools to be more student focused.

The central message of this methodology is student ownership with an emphasis on future-focused, lifelong, technological learning. Students have 24/7 opportunities to engage in online experiences and earn dual credit in high school and college. They include career-related internships led by passionate academic advisors who assist students in self-designing powerful learning environments that eliminate tracking (sorting and selecting based on achievement levels) and practice mixed-ability grouping. This is a model of adapting learning at its best. This is becoming a successful, growing movement due to the fact that students are no longer passive learners but owners of their educational direction.

Personalized learning offers diverse learning events and instructional approaches that are intentionally designed to meet varied interests, academic needs, and cultural influences. As traditional schools begin to explore more 21st century learning opportunities, such as flipped classrooms and various virtual learning options, PBL has become an excellent alternative to strictly paper-and-pencil testing. An example of one district that has authentically invested in competency-based and performance-based learning for all students is the Lindsay Unified School District in California. The essence of their truly amazing journey from an underperforming, traditional K–12 district to a 100 percent performance-based school district can be found on the district website at www.lindsay.k12.ca.us. The multiyear transformation is rooted in the core values they have established (see Lindsay Unified School District, n.d.). The book *Beyond Reform: Systemic Shifts Toward Personalized Learning* (Lindsay Unified School District, 2017) provides more information on this district's success story.

Ponder Box

Choose one of the three following learning profile prompts to discuss in a group of three. Write or think silently, and then be ready to support your opinion with your triad. If you are working alone, choose one prompt to complete independently.

1. In your own words, define *differentiation*, stating its intent and principles.
2. You are a district administrator responsible for launching a movement of differentiation in your school, and you expect all teachers to buy in. To achieve this, the definition, clarity of purpose, and methods are critical. What would this look like in your school?
3. Using a metaphor, analogy, or simile, define where you currently are with differentiation, using a sentence structure such as the following: Differentiation is like a ___________ because ___________.

   For example: Differentiation is like conducting an orchestra. Each musician plays a part in orchestrating good music as a group, but in order to know which musicians need more practice, the conductor needs to hear each player to find out where he or she needs instruction.

Conclusion

Adapting instruction allows all learners equal opportunities within the classroom to acquire the necessary information, make sense of it, and show what they have learned in a way that will best facilitate their own learning needs. It is much more complex than simply reteaching students who didn't get it. Differentiation in its purest form addresses the whole student and specific learning needs. It balances differences in students' readiness, interest, and learning profiles at different times and situations.

Differentiation is not an easy task, but it's the right task. We will never fully know *all* the ways to meet students' needs, year after year, month after month, day after day, hour after hour, minute after minute. Having said that, small steps are normal and perfectly acceptable—as long as the steps move forward. Onward, valued colleagues!

The Takeaways

To adapt and differentiate instruction, consider the following points.

- Differentiated classrooms vary in attitude and structure from more typical traditional classrooms.
- Differentiation adapts learning opportunities in multiple ways to make learning meaningful and attainable for all students and focuses on strong learning objectives and student assessment data.
- Teachers in a differentiated classroom take on a coaching role when designing and guiding students' learning opportunities and activities.
- Teachers can differentiate content, process, product, and learning environment according to students' readiness, interest, or learning profile.
- Teachers use multiple strategies to determine the best learning conditions for students.

CHAPTER 6

MANAGING AND LEADING THE LEARNING

The mind is a powerful thing, isn't it? Our thoughts create a physical reality in both the body and brain that affects our physical and mental well-being. The stories we tell ourselves can either cripple or sabotage change or they can catapult us to new heights of learning. It's our thinking and our attitude, not our DNA, that determine the quality of our lives to a large degree. It's called our *mindset*.

Carol Dweck (2006), a researcher at Stanford University, is well known for her published work on fixed and growth mindsets. A person with a *fixed mindset* believes that each of us has a fixed intellectual capacity and a set amount of talents and abilities that remain static throughout our lifetime. We are what we are through genetics. Those with a *growth mindset*, on the other hand, believe each person has talents, abilities, and intelligences that he or she can develop through effort, strong teaching, and personal persistence. We are what we think we are, and the sky is the limit. Our mindset unconsciously affects how we run and lead a classroom as well as how we instruct, encourage, and respond to students. A key question to ask oneself is, What is my teaching mindset?

We all have our mental image of the role of a teacher. Is it a person who is knowledgeable and able to communicate information to students effectively? Is it a person who is active and unorganized, but students are having a blast? Is it high structure and control? Is it a coach cheering students on to learning? Perhaps the most important role of a teacher in any classroom is to be a leader for students' learning while effectively managing the details of the classroom. There is a significant connection between building student and teacher relationships and learning (Au & Mason, 1981; Brophy, 2008; Cornelius-White, 2007). When learners feel valued and involved, they invest in their environment. On the contrary, when student and adult learners feel disregarded and marginalized, the environmental setting is also affected (Fisher & Frey, 2015).

In this chapter, we explore the role of teachers as classroom leaders and managers as well as the leadership role of teachers and administrators in collaborative work throughout the school or district. We also look at the importance of being present in these roles and building capacity in team dynamics.

Leading and Managing a Classroom

Leading and managing a classroom is not for the faint of heart. They both require a growth mindset, thought, and organization to make them happen consistently. We firmly believe that management and leadership can look like a dictatorship if we have not established the most essential element of any classroom: relationships. Relationships between the teacher and students, and among the students themselves, are the crux of a healthy learning environment.

In figure 6.1, we invite readers to reflect on a quick and efficient checklist for being both the learning leaders *and* managers in their classrooms.

Respond to the following prompts by marking *yes* or *no*.

Leaders	Yes or No	Managers	Yes or No
I have a growth mindset; my students will have many opportunities to succeed through effort, persistence, natural abilities, and talents.		I plan and organize schedules and classroom details for the purpose of consistency and reliability.	
I have a clear vision of where I am going in my classroom.		I prepare materials for myself and students with promptness.	
I share my vision with others and enlist them as team members in achieving the vision.		I purposefully arrange the furniture and the classroom environment for optimal learning conditions.	
I regularly renew my commitment to my vision.		I purposefully orchestrate movement opportunities for my students.	
I celebrate small wins and successes along the learning pathway.		I practice solid routines and procedures that my students can replicate.	

Figure 6.1: Leading and managing practices.

Visit ***go.SolutionTree.com/instruction*** *for a free reproducible version of this figure.*

In the event that a teacher responds "no" to a prompt, keep in mind that the only way we become the leaders, managers, or teachers we are destined to be is to decide who we are to be. A "no" response is honest and provides an opportunity to operate out of a growth mindset and set some personal and professional ways to grow in whatever capacity you choose.

Managers are about mechanics. They know that the devil's in the details. Teachers who are strong classroom managers operate based on the philosophy that the more they plan, organize, and develop systems of routines, the more successfully their classrooms will run, like a well-oiled machine. Leaders are all about developing people. They operate from a philosophy of identifying and addressing student needs (like a physician prescribing a health plan to the patient—a formative assessment) rather than simply assigning a grade—a summative assessment used to sort and select (like a judge delivering a ruling).

Ponder Box

Ponder your leadership or management style and philosophy, and respond to the following three questions.

1. From what mindset do I primarily operate when teaching in my classroom? With colleagues? In the community? In my home?
2. Would I consider myself to be more of a leader or a manager? Neither? Both?
3. Believing that we all operate best in a growth mindset, how will I use this information to lead, manage, or be a stronger teacher?
4. Do I operate more like a prescribing physician or a punitive judge when working directly with students and colleagues?

The Managing Teacher

We have been in classrooms where the lesson plans look wonderful on paper, yet somehow they just do not survive in the classroom. This is largely due to a classroom environment that does not support active learning. Sometimes highly unorganized teachers can impact the learning environment by spending time trying to locate the papers that they were about to pass out, or lacking routines and causing students to wonder how to accomplish the most basic of tasks, such as turning in homework. Perhaps the environment is not healthy for learning because students are afraid to make mistakes because other students and, yes, sometimes even the teacher, will make them feel stupid.

Excellent classroom managers understand that they need to control physical space, routines, and student interactions in order to maximize learning. Gaps of time caused by ineffective routines lead to off-task behaviors. We also recognize how undesirable student interactions can often lead to the destruction of learning. Figure 6.2 asks teachers to think about their current management areas and strategies.

Directions: For each management area, list your current strategies and how they are working for you and your students.

Management Area	Current Strategies	Reflection on Strategies
1. Assigning groups or tasks		
2. Distributing materials or papers		
3. Collecting materials or papers		
4. Managing disruptive behavior (blurting out)		
5. Managing off-task behavior		
6. Managing mistreatment of peers		
7. Other		

Figure 6.2: Management strategies reflection sheet.

Visit ***go.SolutionTree.com/instruction*** *for a free reproducible version of this figure.*

Knowing when and how to establish routines and intervene with disruptive behaviors is part of the artistry of teaching. The following list offers a few strategies for each of these areas.

- Assigning groups or tasks:
    - Create *standing groups* that meet periodically. These groups are set up in advance and revisited over a period of time such as a grading period, hence the term *standing*. The benefit of having

standing groups is that when a teacher gives the name of a group (for example, "get with your blue group"), students know with whom to meet, and quickly get together. Standing group names and configurations can change after each grading period or any other shorter or longer time frame during the school year.

- Deliberately assign working groups for a specific task or activity, and post these group configurations with a document camera or on a PowerPoint slide. Include not only who is in each group but also where in the room they should sit.
- If students sit in groups of four, assign each student within the group a color, for example: blue, red, purple, and green. The teacher can then create various pairings within the group by calling color combinations for them to form pairs (for example, blues with purples and reds with greens). Teachers can also use this to form larger classroom groups (such as gathering in the four corners of the room based on designated colors).
- Create a culture that encourages all students to work with each other over time. The classroom culture should establish that students will have the opportunity to work with and learn from everyone else in the room at some point. The exception to this is if there are specific discipline issues that prevent student learning. Groups are flexible and purposeful based on the intention of the activity or task.

- Distributing materials or papers:
    - Assign rotating materials managers. Materials managers are responsible for gathering and returning any classroom materials needed for tasks.
    - If students sit in rows, pass papers across the row instead of front to back or back to front. This enables students to look at the person to whom they hand the papers, instead of trying to hand the papers behind their back or hitting the person in front of them on the back of the head with the papers. We have never seen a stack of papers dropped and scattered when being passed sideways, but we have often seen papers not making the pass the other way! If students sit in pods, have a folder for each pod in the middle of the group of desks or table, and return papers to the folders for students to collect as they sit down.
    - Have a central materials location, such as stacking drawers or specific bins that provide a common area for students to gather and return materials.
    - Designate a specific area near the classroom door where students pick up any handouts for the class as they enter. In elementary classrooms, teachers can do this during transitions from morning meetings to the first subject area, between subjects, or when students enter the room from special classes or lunch.
    - Have a specific folder where students pick up any handouts they missed from being absent. Secondary teachers could consider color-coding their classes so that students know which folder or stacking bin to check for work based on their class period.
- Collecting materials or papers:
    - Assign classroom collectors who will collect assignments throughout the class as necessary. These may overlap with materials managers, but classroom collectors specifically collect items such as permission slips or other class papers or documents in a folder.
    - As with distributing papers, if students sit in rows, pass papers across the row instead of front to back or back to front. Students will be able to see the person giving them the papers, and this movement is smoother, faster, and prevents papers from being dropped.

    - If students sit in pods, have a group folder in the center of the group of desks or table with a checklist stapled to the inside that includes names of the students in the group. Then a designated checker collects the papers from the group and labels the column of the assignment he or she is collecting, then checks off who has turned in the assignment. All papers go into the folder, and the teacher can pick up the papers from the folders at the end of class.
    - Have a specific drawer, folder, or bin where students turn in their work at the beginning of class or when the teacher prompts them.
- Managing disruptive behavior (such as blurting out):
    - Have a private conversation with the student about the behavior. Sometimes the student is not even aware of what he or she is doing. For example, ask the student to explain why it is necessary to blurt out in class. Is the student feeling unrecognized? Frustrated because he or she wants to share but can't? Or is it truly lack of control?
    - Give the student five or so toothpicks (or any other object) to act as a counter. Each time the student blurts, remove one toothpick. This will focus the student on the behavior. After all toothpicks have run out, the student must remain silent for the rest of the whole-class session. The goal is to narrow down the amount of the toothpicks until eliminating them completely, and teach self-control and awareness in the process.
    - Use turn and talks frequently. This gives the student an opportunity to voice his or her opinion and hear someone else's.
    - Use a stop and jot before any discussions. This will encourage students to think before speaking.
- Managing off-task behavior:
    - Perhaps the most basic strategy is proximity. Think about how a person might drive when he or she sees a police car in the rearview mirror. As teachers get closer to students, they remind them to get to work.
    - If students are working in groups, check in frequently to monitor them. Working in groups is a privilege, not a right. If learning cannot occur for a student in the group, he or she needs to have different working conditions. Separate the student and provide clear expectations for completing the work.
    - Check the pace of learning. It is possible that repetition, long pauses, or too much time on a single structure, task, or activity is promoting the off-task behavior because of developmental attention spans.
    - Use preferential seating and close monitoring.
    - Develop personal cues with the student to call attention to the behavior without calling the student out in public.
    - Ask self-correcting questions rather than giving behavior statements (especially negative statements).
    - Above all else, do not get into a power struggle. Teachers will lose every time.
- Managing mistreatment of peers:
    - Treat all students with kindness, patience, and respect. Teachers should model the behaviors they want to see.

- Build the classroom environment around appreciating differences (not just accepting differences) and what respect looks like, feels like, and sounds like. Have frequent classroom meetings to discuss the class climate and how well everyone is learning together.
- Use one-on-one feedback, and do not publicly reprimand students.
- Remind students that everyone is here to learn, and no one has the right to prevent anyone else from learning.
- Listen to both sides of the story. Reprimand and provide appropriate and consistent consequences to a student mistreating another student. Teachers can develop an escalating consequence list with the class. For example, it could begin with recognizing wrongdoing and verbally apologizing, with a next step of writing apologies and exploring suggestions for conflict resolutions, then progressing to calling parents and involving administrators, and finally, implementing administrative decisions about broader consequences.

We recommend that teachers develop classroom agreements (we call them *agreements* rather than *rules*) with students so that there is greater buy-in. However, even when classroom agreements are developed together, there can still be breakdowns of behavior. Figures 6.3, 6.4, 6.5, 6.6 (page 116), and 6.7 (page 116) provide templates for planning additional strategies and tools to manage behaviors in the classroom. Figure 6.3 allows teachers to reflect on strategies that can be implemented to help prevent breakdowns of classroom rules and plan steps and strategies for when there is a breakdown. Preplanning these strategies and steps will help avoid in-the-moment reactions or inconsistently implementing consequences.

List the behavior agreements for your class in section 1. Then determine what strategies or interventions could be used to promote appropriate behavior in section 2. Finally, if the rules are broken, what steps will be consistently taken? List these in section 3.

1. The agreements for the class are the following.
   a.
   b.
   c.
   d.
   e.
2. I will use these three strategies to prevent possible problems.
   a.
   b.
   c.
3. This is the recourse I will take when a student violates agreements.
   a. First step:
   b. Second step:
   c. Third step:

Figure 6.3: Prevention as intervention template.

Visit ***go.SolutionTree.com/instruction*** *for a free reproducible version of this figure.*

Figure 6.4 provides a checklist for students to self-monitor their weekly behavior. This is given to students to self-evaluate their classroom behavior and relationships.

Actions	Monday	Tuesday	Wednesday	Thursday	Friday
I begin class on time.	Yes No	Yes No	Yes No	Yes No	Yes No
I am ready for class with my books and supplies.	Yes No	Yes No	Yes No	Yes No	Yes No
I obey class rules.	Yes No	Yes No	Yes No	Yes No	Yes No
I treat others how I want to be treated.	Yes No	Yes No	Yes No	Yes No	Yes No
I actively participate in class activities.	Yes No	Yes No	Yes No	Yes No	Yes No
I keep my hands and feet to myself.	Yes No	Yes No	Yes No	Yes No	Yes No
I keep my personal space organized.	Yes No	Yes No	Yes No	Yes No	Yes No
Other behaviors:	Yes No	Yes No	Yes No	Yes No	Yes No

Student signature: ______________________ Parent signature: ______________________

Teacher signature: ______________________

When I have reached 85 percent of my goal, this will be my reward: ______________________

Figure 6.4: Tracking my behavior template.

Visit ***go.SolutionTree.com/instruction*** *for a free reproducible version of this figure.*

Figure 6.5 is a checklist for monitoring student behavior. The top is usually checked by the teacher, and both student and teacher reflect on the observation. This form addresses both the student's strengths and areas to grow and stretch.

Name: ______________________ Date: __________ Teacher: ______________________

Part 1: Strength Areas

_______ I complete my work.

_______ I show respect for myself and others.

_______ I show leadership.

_______ I participate fully.

_______ I am prepared for class.

_______ I use time wisely.

_______ I follow class rules.

_______ I am reliable.

_______ I am honest.

_______ I work persistently.

Part 2: Stretch Areas

_______ I am uncooperative.

_______ I blurt out or disrupt class.

_______ I am disrespectful of others' space.

_______ Other: ______________

_______ I am off task.

_______ I have incomplete work.

_______ I have problems listening.

_______ Other: ______________

Student reflection:

Teacher reflection:

Figure 6.5: My behavior progress-report template.

Visit ***go.SolutionTree.com/instruction*** *for a free reproducible version of this figure.*

Choosing the Consequences lists possible consequences for breaking classroom agreements. Students or the teacher can choose the consequences for inappropriate behavior as well as rewards for on-task behaviors in advance. Figure 6.6 provides a template.

The following options are consequences for disruptive behavior.

______ Time-out area in the room

______ Time-out area in a designated room

______ Forgive Me, Please slip

______ Closed suspension; no social interaction with others

______ Lunch detention (work through lunch)

______ Recess withheld (work through recess)

______ Loss of specific privileges list: ______

______ Contact parent or guardian

______ Behavior contract

______ Other: ____________________

The following options are rewards for on-task behavior.

______ Pride in yourself

______ Music of choice with headset

______ Computer time

______ Mentor in another classroom

______ Special seating (sofa or comfortable chair)

______ Other: ____________________

______ Good news note

______ Star student recognition

______ Leadership opportunities

______ Positive postcard from office

Student signature: ______________________________ Parent signature: ______________________________

Teacher signature: ______________________________ Date: ______________________________

Figure 6.6: Choosing the Consequences template.

Visit ***go.SolutionTree.com/instruction*** *for a free reproducible version of this figure.*

When students are involved in their own plan of action to correct a classroom infraction, we are creating citizens who take responsibility for their own actions. The Forgive Me, Please template (figure 6.7) gives the student a framework for identifying the problem, who else was involved, and what future actions he or she will commit to exhibiting as he or she moves forward.

Name: ____ Date: ____________________

Others involved: ____

1. I acted inappropriately when I . . .

2. Looking back at the incident, now I know I should have . . .

3. I hurt other people around me by . . .

4. This is what I'd like to say to make things right.

5. Specific behaviors I will commit to are . . .

Student signature: ______________________________ Parent signature: ______________________________

Teacher signature: ______________________________

Figure 6.7: Forgive Me, Please template.

Visit ***go.SolutionTree.com/instruction*** *for a free reproducible version of this figure.*

Ponder Box

Revisit your strategy list from figure 6.2 (page 111). What other strategies might you want to try? Make a new list of possible strategies to try, or add them in a different color to your responses in figure 6.2.

Teachers can establish consistent routines in which they manage inclusive activities for all students in the classroom throughout the entire year. However, not all strategies work 100 percent of the time. It can be very frustrating and is often a process of trial and error. Of course, the stronger the relationship a teacher has with students, the easier this process is. A smoothly running classroom will facilitate learning leadership, as well.

The Leading Teacher

Teachers who lead learning create an environment where learning is safe and students feel accepted. They build solid relationships with their students and understand what students need to learn as well as how they learn. They promote growth mindsets in their students and encourage all students to invest their efforts into learning and to value mistakes. Leading teachers create opportunities for all students to work together in various configurations over time. In these classrooms, all students cheer for and support each other in learning. This does not happen naturally; the leading teacher deliberately orchestrates and maintains the learning environment.

To lead both in the classroom and as a systems team requires educators to use their most powerful tool, which is knowing *why* they collectively do what they do. Consider for a moment Simon Sinek's (2009a) Golden Circle of effectiveness. In the center of the Golden Circle rests the compelling *why*, or purpose for what we do, surrounded by *how* we accomplish the goal, while the outer layer of the circle dictates specifically *what* we will do to accomplish our task.

Specifically, in the classroom, the why defines our attitudes toward, beliefs about, and commitments to learning, students, parents, the political public, and, most powerfully, our commitment to be our best selves on behalf of all audiences. In the age of the Common Core and similar standards, the *why* is fueled by the fact that standards of excellence will ensure that the 21st century student is college and career ready and able to compete successfully in the global economy. The *how* is the action plan to get to our goal; the backward planning of the standards into specific daily learning tasks. This also requires that we leverage our instructional time wisely. Unfortunately, districts that have not fully understood the how have attempted to accomplish their goals by testing, testing, testing! The overabundance and poor planning of assessment simply does not align with the why of education. Classroom management, teaching style, and specific and explicit lesson design influence how leading teachers teach. Our actions to encourage students to love learning and want to come back every day—empowering, nurturing, planning, reading, writing, explaining, bargaining, and deeply thinking—define the what of education. When we do it well, it is unstoppable. Sinek's (2009b) argument is that students, adults, and the public at large are not inspired by the what. Overwhelmingly, they respond to the intentional, purposeful why. Figure 6.8 (page 118) asks readers to consider, reflect, and act on several famous quotes about the why of education.

Directions: After reading each quote, reflect on its significance, and make notes as to how you would apply it in your professional life.

Quote	Significance	Application
"There are risks and costs to a program of action. But they are far less than the long-range risks and costs of comfortable inaction." —John F. Kennedy		
"Students should not only be trained to live in a democracy when they grow up; they should have the chance to live in one today." —Alfie Kohn		
"Any situation in which some individuals prevent others from engaging in the process of inquiry is one of violence. The means used are not important; to alienate human beings from their own decision-making is to change them into objects." —Paulo Freire		
"It is because modern education is so seldom inspired by a great hope that it so seldom achieves great results. The wish to preserve the past rather than the hope of creating the future dominates the minds of those who control the teaching of the young." —Bertrand Russell		
"Education should not be the filling of a pail, but the lighting of a fire." —William Butler Yeats		
"Where, after all, do universal human rights begin? In small places, close to home—so close and so small they cannot be seen on any maps of the world. Yet they are the world of the individual person. . . . Such are the places where every man, woman, and child seeks equal justice, equal opportunity, equal dignity without discrimination. Unless these rights have meaning there, they have little meaning anywhere. Without concerned citizen action to uphold them close to home, we shall look in vain for progress in the larger world." —Eleanor Roosevelt		
"The more we increase the active participation and partnership with young people, the better we serve them. . . . And the more comprehensively we work with them as service partners, the more we increase our public value to the entire community." —Carmen Martinez		

Figure 6.8: Reflection sheet of quotes on the why of education.

Visit ***go.SolutionTree.com/instruction*** *for a free reproducible version of this figure.*

Being Present

Leading teachers and administrators are first and foremost present in every context of their job. We think of being present in the sense that not only are our bodies present, but our entire minds are present as well. This includes situations in the classroom, staff meetings, collaborative team meetings, parent meetings, and every other time we are in our personal and professional roles. We live in an age where it is common to claim we are multitasking when in fact we are exhibiting off-task behaviors. The reality is that we cannot focus on two things at once, even though we are able to switch between two things very quickly! Being present in professional situations means that we are attuned to every conversation and event in the moment.

We create the ideal learning climate in a classroom by being intensely aware of and responsible for our actions, which fosters a growth mindset, allows us to constructively address behavior disruptions and student disagreements, and ensures we understand the why of establishing healthy learning environments, one task and one focus at a time. Being present is taking full responsibility for the choices we make in life. It is the lens you use to focus on *now*, not the past or future. When we focus on the past or the future, it is easy for our focus to become riddled with comparisons and judgments.

In these interactions, a teacher who is both a leader and manager of learning has a role with other teachers that is also crucial. In examining the leadership role teachers have within collaborative teams, reflect on whether you would prefer to have a coach or a director. Coaching implies being in the trenches as a worker bee with fellow colleagues to explore solutions together, and maximizing the talents and skills of every individual on the team. Conversely, directors dictate orders while their colleagues deliver. This kind of leadership leaves little room for autonomy and most assuredly leads to disenfranchised team members and marginalized relationships (Bosworth, 2016). Leaders who choose to be present and have open communication build trust rapidly and become respected, go-to co-laborers.

Building Capacity in Team Dynamics

Peter Senge's (2006) book *The Fifth Discipline: The Art and Practice of the Learning Organization* is a popular resource to build capacity in team dynamics. His premise is that learning organizations must include all stakeholders in decision making and implementation. Senge (2006) contends that when groups dialogue well, they learn trust, reliability, and productivity. In addition, they are less likely to be derailed by members in the minority who choose not work collaboratively with others. Senge (2006) classifies team communication practices into four categories: (1) telling, (2) observing, (3) asking, and (4) having skillful discussion. He further notes the levels of advocacy and inquiry inherent in each category. *Inquiry* is the request of information—a query or investigation for the purpose of clarity gained through asking questions. *Advocacy* is the support or recommendation given to a cause or concern. Advocates champion the efforts of the people they serve. Both high advocacy and high inquiry exist on a healthy team. As teacher teams meet to champion their efforts and ask clarifying questions, the goal of skillful discussion is reached when there is a balance created between advocacy and inquiry.

1. **Telling (high advocacy, low inquiry):** We expect to find people in leadership roles who are "tellers" because they are the primary decision makers and leaders in the school. However, if the teller is all about top-down leadership tactics without listening to the people who surround him or her, teachers will often resist. Extreme tellers like to bulldoze others with their opinions and offer little in the way of listening to differing opinions. In a healthy dynamic, the teller provides direction and seeks to build capacity by instructing, supporting, and listening.
2. **Observing (low advocacy, low inquiry):** Observers have opinions, but they express them with trusted colleagues outside the team setting. Some observers are simply quiet processors while others need more time to process, so they observe first before they engage. Some observers choose not to be involved and are disinterested and disengaged because they don't feel heard or validated by their team.
3. **Asking (low advocacy, high inquiry):** This person needs time to ask numerous questions to gain clarity. They think of scenarios that others may not take time to address and can be excellent people to address tough issues as long as they move to a solution. On the other hand, the extreme asker can

be a negative voice that sabotages a team by asking so many questions that he or she shuts down action by creating doubt and fear.

4. **Having skillful discussion (high advocacy, high inquiry):** When a team commits to skillful dialogue, members are intent on listening to one another and ask the tough questions that need to be asked. Conflict is expected, but skilled discussers seek consensus and informed decisions that benefit all.

Figure 6.9 illustrates these items in quadrants that progress toward the team goal of skillful discussion, with high inquiry and high advocacy.

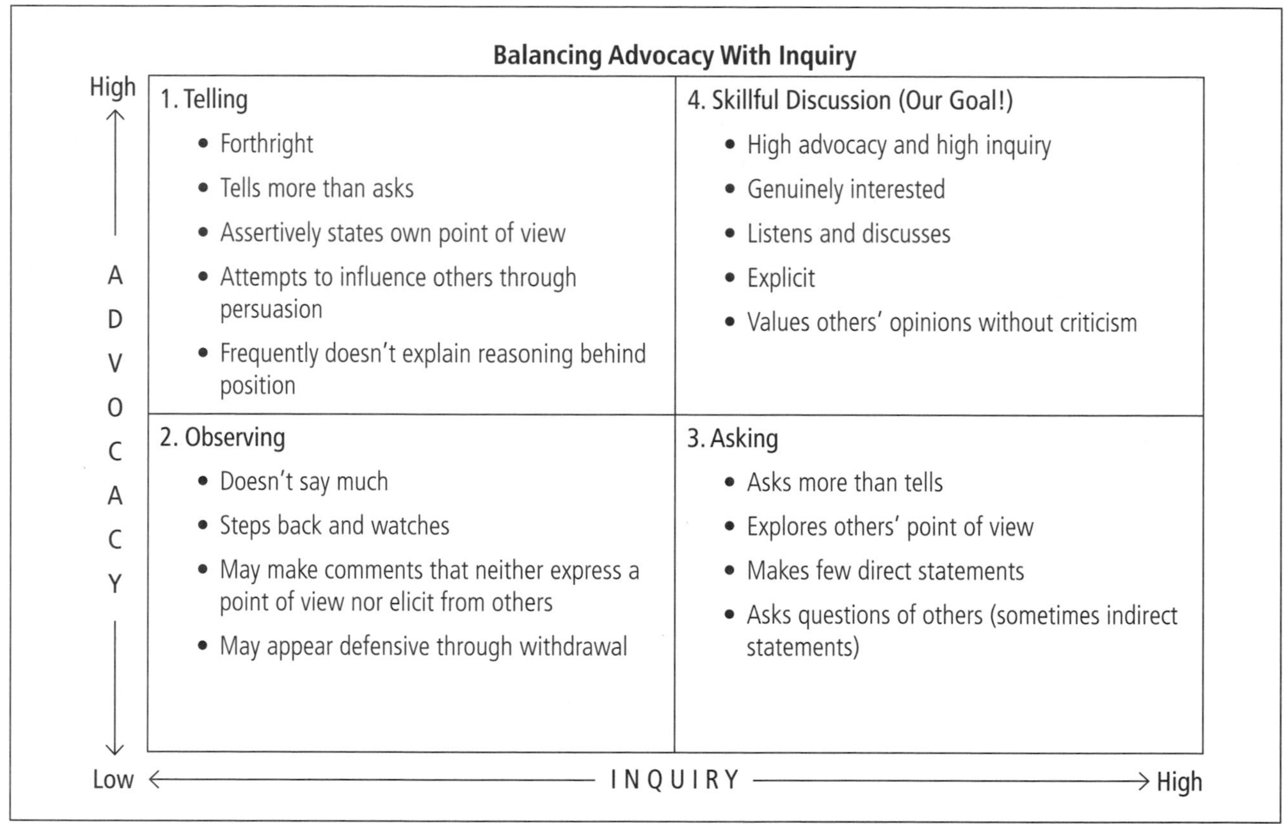

Source: Senge, 2006.

Figure 6.9: Inquiry and advocacy conversations.

Discussing can appear to be like percussing, as in a percussion instrument that makes a loud sound, but it may or may not be playing in full harmony with the other instruments. In a team meeting, often there can be banter back and forth until the strongest voice holds out for the win, rather than the most effective idea winning. Mature teams seek *skillful* discussion over traditional discussion, which typically tends to be about advocacy rather than inquiry.

Teams never accomplish skillful discussion on its own, though some dialogue may be part of the process. The purpose of skillful discussion is to make an informed decision, challenge assumptions, and put an action plan in place through agreement. Teams use dialogue the most when innovation and experimentation are their goals. It is from dialogue that ideas take root. Figure 6.10 serves as a guide to identify the types of conversations that can take place in healthy and unhealthy team discussions.

	Healthy Advocacy	Unhealthy Advocacy	Healthy Inquiry	Unhealthy Inquiry
Teller	"As leader of the team, I believe it is important that these behaviors are consistently exhibited as we work together. I invite your input at all times in order to make our work together as productive as it can be."	"I don't care what the group thinks. Just let me close my door and do what I was hired to do! I have been successful doing what I have been doing for years, and I am not about to give that up now!"	"What are the most pressing concerns of the group? Please be candid and explicit with your needs. How can we support one another?"	"This autonomy stuff is too time consuming! What's in it for me?"
Observer	"I appreciate that the team knows it takes me longer to process. After listening to others on the team and staff, I am clear on the expectations and ready to move ahead with an informed decision that will benefit students and staff."	"It's clear to me that my opinions are not valued here, so I will keep them to myself."	"I have been observing some of the other teams in action, and I am wondering if we have considered . . . . What are your thoughts?"	"No comment!" "I don't have anything to add."
Asker	"Have we considered how this decision will affect the other teams in the school?"	"Let's make a decision here! Others may not like our plan, but isn't it most important that we do what's best for us? Come on! Let's move!"	"Before I can move to a decision, I need to have these questions answered. Can you help me understand this thinking? I am confused."	"We can't do this because . . . ." "What will happen if . . . ?" "Do you realize how crippling this is going to be?" "What is the teachers' union going to say?"
Skillful Discusser	"Since we represent our school and team, I think it is important to survey the staff and students to see what is in their best interest before we move ahead."		"What do you feel might be our greatest strengths and weaknesses? What solutions can we create to become a stronger team?"	

Figure 6.10: Healthy and unhealthy conversations.

Senge, Kleiner, Roberts, Ross, & Smith (1994) suggest that the purpose behind building a team is to develop a sense of shared belief and meaning. Sometimes words fall short when team members understand things differently. When teams make decisions quickly for the sake of efficiency but do not ensure all members' clarity, effectiveness will suffer. Leaving a meeting with a vague understanding leads to criticism and confusion.

If a team member leaves a meeting angry, frustrated, or confused, he or she should ask, "Why am I feeling this way? What is the condition of my thinking?" When these feelings emerge, say, "When the group is saying ________________, I find myself confused and in disagreement because ________________." Teams that listen to the *because* gain clarity and deeper trust. When a disagreement arises, the following questions provide an opportunity to come to a solution to the problem rather than dig a rut through complaint and frustration.

- What are the exact *facts* of the situation?
- What *methods* will we use to solve this?
- What is the collective *goal*?
- What do we *value*? What is the right thing to do?

Whether or not teachers have the good fortune to teach in a school or district with an administrator who knows how to effectively lead, the responsibility for building a healthy school culture where skillful discussion is the norm lies within each individual on the team, whatever the role. Teachers need not wait for the administrator to intervene before taking positive action for themselves and within their classrooms. It does, however, certainly make unity and systems thinking much more attainable when the leader shows the way.

Teachers leading the work without administrative backing can be futile, and others may even view it as sabotage or misappropriated authority. Even when a teacher is a natural leader, having a leading administrator to support, connect, and protect his or her intentions is the best-case scenario. Administrators must be the lead learners who model delegation and staff empowerment. Every faculty needs an administrator who models the expected behavior before releasing leadership responsibilities to others. If procedures run awry, teachers need to feel they are supported and not hung out to dry on their own.

Teachers need to be leaders of learning in their classrooms and every other aspect of their professional lives. Teaching in a school or district with administrators who also lead learning greatly enhances their efforts. In the next section, we examine just how administrators can be leaders of learning.

Ponder Box

We would love it if all teams worked collectively and productively. Unfortunately, we know this is not always the case. When team members do not function well with one another, we recommend they consider the following three questions to begin to understand the dynamics of the team.

1. Which quadrant do I most operate out of when I am working with my team or colleagues?
2. Where would my colleagues place me?
3. If skillful discussion is our school goal, where are we now? If we are not there yet, what deliberate steps will we take to operate with skillful discussion regularly?

The Leading Administrator

We expect leading administrators in today's schools not only to lead and inspire a diverse staff to achieve high standards of academic excellence but also to articulate a clear vision. Reaching the vision is done through effective, strategic thinking with a leadership team first and then articulated to the collaborative teams (or all leaders and teachers if the school or district does not have teams) to create alignment to the system's vision and also to create a sense of autonomy for teachers. When relationships are deepened with key community partnerships, the school's mission will expand. When outside sources have a direct line to the decision makers, greater commitment and innovation result. Further, being a strong leader requires staying abreast of current best practices through professional reading, conferences, and rich opportunities.

Administrators who manage and lead successfully also acknowledge the importance of hearing the voices of their staff. One of the best resources we recommend for leading and managing systemic collaboration is *The Five Disciplines of PLC Leaders* by Timothy D. Kanold (2011). Kanold outlines the importance of growing emotional intelligence. For some leaders, relationship building can be very unnatural, yet they cannot establish effective teams without it. Leaders who exude emotional intelligence are ones who regularly create a positive climate by praising often, giving direction and support, constructively criticizing, and framing the group's mission.

Whether we want to admit it, emotions weigh heavily on things we think, say, and do. Though we'd like to believe that most decisions are made with rationality and the use of logic and data, they are impacted by personal value systems and the lessons learned from past experiences in our lives (Walton, 2012). Emotionally intelligent people are ones who know themselves well, have a handle on their passions, and in the face of crisis are able to remain grounded and mindful of others and themselves.

Stress can be a major player in the way we react emotionally, as well. The way we cope or our failure to cope is largely dependent upon our emotional intelligence. Sometimes we do not have a choice about the kinds of people we work alongside, but we do have control over the way we react and adapt our behavior to retain a positive perspective on issues that arise in the workplace. Table 6.1 gives some examples of reactions to stressors that are either healthy and adaptive (indicating emotional intelligence) or unhealthy and maladaptive.

Table 6.1: Healthy and Unhealthy Reactions to Stressors

Stressors	Healthy, Adaptive Behavior	Unhealthy, Maladaptive Behavior
Feels overworked	Delegates responsibility	Accepts overload, and performance deteriorates
Is uncertain about a policy or situation	Finds out what the policy is and seeks a solution	Guesses inappropriately and gets angry or frustrated
Is involved in a poor working relationship	Raises issue with a colleague and negotiates for a better relationship	Attacks colleagues indirectly through a third party
Chooses wrong career path	Leaves the profession for one more suited to his or her skills and personality	Loses confidence and becomes convinced of own inadequacy
Invests in work versus family	Revisits priorities and negotiates a balance of work and family	Blames organization and colleagues for problems and discontent
Feels role ambiguity	Seeks clarification with boss and colleagues	Becomes reactive, uncertain, toxic, or confused

Source: Adapted from Walton, 2012.

The reality exists that when our emotions are intact, healthier workplace relationships are the result. In the next section, we focus on productive team activities to strengthen adult relationships leading to improved productivity, joy, and balance in the workplace.

Activities for Collaborative Team Building

We provide the following activities for teams to begin building the foundation of a high-performing school culture through collaboration and systems thinking.

Exploring the Six Domains of Highly Effective Schools

We invite you to consider six highly developed domains present in effective schools: (1) assessment, (2) instruction, (3) curriculum, (4) reflection, (5) collaboration, and (6) physical environment. We offer the following exercise for single departments or the whole school staff to use to build consensus, team autonomy, and shared systemwide vision. The benefit of this activity is twofold.

1. It allows everyone the opportunity to buy into the process of strategic planning in a very user-friendly manner that is not driven from the top down.
2. Everyone's voice is heard in a collaborative setting and the investment is much more profound. This is an excellent tool for groups who typically have not created a common picture together and whose communications across grade levels and content areas are limited.

The six steps of this activity are as follows.

1. Count off from 1 to 6 and divide the staff evenly into the following domains: assessment, instruction, curriculum, reflection, collaboration, and physical environment.
2. Prompt each group with the following question: What does best practice look like in your specific domain? Pull out all the stops. Dream big. If you could have the ideal school in which to teach, what would your domain look like?
3. Give each group chart paper, and ask members to brainstorm and collect all the suggested ideas (five to fifteen minutes).
4. Once all the ideas are on the table, the group now begins to prioritize the best thinking that has emerged from the brainstorming session (five minutes). As the priorities are being discussed, participants use the template in figure 6.11 to record them in the column that represents their domain. The first three columns appear on one side of an 8.5 x 11 sheet of paper. The remaining three columns appear on the back side of the paper.
5. Prioritize the responses and share in a gallery walk. Allow others to add to the initial brainstorm on the chart paper (ten to fifteen minutes).
6. Once each group has had the opportunity to review and add input to each other's domain lists, they go back to their original domain and begin to develop a three- to five-year (or three-phase) systems plan.

Instruction	Assessment	Curriculum

Collaboration	Reflection	Physical Environment

Figure 6.11: Six domains of highly effective schools.

Visit ***go.SolutionTree.com/instruction*** *to access a free reproducible version of this figure.*

Identifying Mission, Vision, Values, and Goals

A mission statement should be concise and repeatable, and everyone affiliated with the school should commit to carrying it through. The purpose of developing the mission is to answer the question, Why do we exist?

The vision statement supports the mission by answering the question, What do we hope to become? A simple yet effective way to get to the vision is to complete the activity for the six domains of highly effective schools (figure 6.11). From those entries, teams can create a big-picture plan and include everyone's voice in the final picture. The vision is like presenting an empty canvas to the participants and letting each add to the final picture on the canvas.

The values speak directly to the moral imperatives in our work and answer the questions, What do we believe or value in our workplace? What attitudes, behaviors, and commitments (ABCs) are we willing to make to one another? If we believe these things are important, what actions can we expect from ourselves and coworkers? This leads to the goals, which answer the question, What specific actions must we take to reach the mission, vision, and values? The following section discusses how teams can effectively set goals.

Setting SMART Goals

SMART goals are strategic and specific, measurable, attainable, results oriented, and time bound (Conzemius & O'Neill, 2014). Teachers can use the template in figure 6.12 as a universal tool to set SMART goals by classroom, department or grade level, school, or district.

Team Name: ______ Team Leader: ______ Team Members: ______				
Team SMART Goal	**Strategies and Action Steps**	**Who Is Responsible**	**Target Date or Timeline**	**Evidence of Effectiveness**

Figure 6.12: SMART goals template.

Visit ***go.SolutionTree.com/instruction*** *for a free reproducible version of this figure.*

Discovering Strengths Compass Activity

This is an excellent activity for building culture with laughter and engagement, and understanding how we all work in different ways and with diverse personalities. School Reform Initiative (SRI) published a version of this activity online and notes that it was "developed in the field by educators" (School Reform Initiative, 2007). To do this activity, engage in the following six steps.

1. Describe to the team the personality characteristics of each of the following directions.
   a. **North (doers):** These people are action oriented and like to get things done quickly. They are usually early implementers and like to be where the new, innovative ideas are happening.
   b. **South (feelers):** These people crave peace and harmony in the workplace. They like to hear everyone's opinion before they make a decision.
   c. **East (speculators):** These people need to know the big picture before they make a decision. They rarely act before taking considerable time to examine all the angles.
   d. **West (detailers):** These people are all business. They want the who, what, when, and where, and then to be left to get to the task. Efficiency and accuracy are of utmost importance.
2. Using figure 6.13 (page 126), have teachers determine which direction best describes who they are when making decisions with their team. Assign four areas in the room for each of the directions to process together. If there are large numbers of people in each group, make several groups within the same direction. For example, twenty-one northerners would split off into three groups of seven. The smaller the group, the more dialogue will take place. The ideal group size is six to eight members.
3. Each direction answers the following questions together (fifteen to twenty minutes).
   a. What are the greatest strengths of your direction?
   b. What are your greatest weaknesses?
   c. Which direction do you have greatest difficulty working with, and why?
   d. What do other directions need to know about you to build a more collaborative school culture?
4. Bring the whole group back together, and ask individuals to share their responses. In essence, this activity is a common assessment of the school culture. Listen very carefully to the language each group uses to begin to understand why conflict happens in the workplace. It typically isn't that we don't like the people we work with; they simply see and perform in different ways. The facilitator needs to capture how many people each group represents. For example, with seventy-two teachers, you may have fifteen in the north, ten in the south, thirty in the west, and seventeen in the east.

Looking at the numbers, what are your strengths and weaknesses? Are each of the compass directions balanced in number? Take the following school scenario for example. Out of seventy-two total staff, only fifteen are risk takers and innovators (north). Over half (forty-seven) are detail-oriented (west) and slow to act (east). The remaining ten are committed to group consensus and building harmony (south). Variety is important in any school, so representation from each group is needed when putting committees or teams together.

5. After each direction has had an opportunity to share, we recommend taking a picture of each of the four groups and posting it in the faculty lounge or a place where decision making is going on so learning styles are validated and understood.
6. When teams get stuck, northern thinking can move them forward. When conflict arises, the southerners are the buffer to the other directions. When detailed planning is required, westerners are the best leads. Easterners typically ask questions that others do not think about, so they become great partners for addressing the why.

This is a great activity to do with students as well for teachers who are launching differentiation or building community at the start of a new school year.

	Strengths	Weaknesses	Most Difficult Direction for Us, and Why	What Others Need to Know About Us	Reflections
North "Let's put action to our ideas! Let's move forward."					
South "I am all about harmony and hearing everyone's voice."					
East "I need time to think about the big picture before I move ahead. Show me why."					
West "Give me the details: who, what, when, and where?"					

Figure 6.13: Compass activity template.

Visit ***go.SolutionTree.com/instruction*** *for a free reproducible version of this figure.*

Understanding Team Dynamics Activity

As we saw with Senge's (2006) communication classifications, each role within team dynamics has strengths that can also manifest as weaknesses if not used constructively. For teams that are having difficulty coming to consensus, we provide the template in figure 6.14 to help keep them on a constructive path.

However, this template can be used for many purposes, including:

- Formative assessment to determine what students have learned and where to go next
- Team processing
- Conflict resolution
- Common assessment disaggregation

For teams planning specific action steps to improve their functioning, users should be specific about expected team behaviors.

Data + Collaboration = Results		
What? What do the data say factually?	**So What?** What conclusions or inferences might you draw from the facts?	**Now What?** What action steps will you take?

a. What do the data tell us?

b. What are the patterns? What stands out?

c. What questions do you have?

Figure 6.14: What, So What, Now What? template.

Visit ***go.SolutionTree.com/instruction*** *for a free reproducible version of this figure.*

In Jim Collins's (2001) book *Good to Great*, he uses a window-mirror metaphor to examine effective companies seeking greater success. He found that strong organizations look in the mirror and freely give credit directly to the team when things are going well, and they become experts in taking responsibility for their actions when the opposite happens. Though the mirror is vital as we examine ways to improve, being fixated on it can inflate egos and cause teachers and leaders to forget how they got to the pinnacle of their careers. Likewise, the obsession of looking out the window too frequently can lead to a scattered focus on too many ideas and initiatives, whereas forgetting to look out the window leaves no room for new innovation and possibility. The power is in creating a hybrid of the two. Figure 6.15 (page 128) offers a survey to collect data regarding school climate.

Conclusion

Leading, managing, and working collaboratively is not always an easy task, whether in a classroom, within a team, or at the school or district level. Expecting individuals to be sharp, perky, and optimistic on command as they work together every day of the school year is not always realistic. This work requires all of us to roll up our sleeves and make the best effort we can to be servant leaders to one another. It's not always an easy task, but it's the right task. Our students are the future, and the messages we send, whether positive or negative, impact them and ourselves.

Working together to create a growth mindset that fosters a positive school climate not only mitigates bullying, suspensions, absenteeism, and substance abuse but it increases academic, social, and emotional

School Culture Audit

Monitoring the Journey

Respond to the following prompts by assigning a number between 1 and 5.

1	2	3	4	5
Awareness but no use	Beginning to use	Routine practice	Routine practice and beginning refinement	Established use and ongoing refinement

1. Teachers in my school are clear on our mission and are committed to ensuring students learn at high levels.
   1 2 3 4 5
2. The culture of our school is positive, upbeat, and student centered.
   1 2 3 4 5
3. Our school is committed to results rather than random intentions through the use of common assessments.
   1 2 3 4 5
4. Teachers value working together consistently as a systems team across all grade levels with a laser focus on student learning.
   1 2 3 4 5
5. We study and discuss assessment and grading to provide a consistent message for our student and parent populations.
   1 2 3 4 5
6. We collect accurate data as a progress-monitoring tool to ensure early intervention, enrichment, and differentiation to meet the diverse needs of our students.
   1 2 3 4 5
7. We take intentional time to reflect and celebrate school strengths and stretch goals in order to promote a continual cycle of school improvement.
   1 2 3 4 5

Consensus Survey

Respond to the following questions.

1. What are the strengths of our school?

2. Where do we need to grow; where do we need to change practices?

3. What are our priorities?

4. What is one thing we need to do *now* to change our practices?

After the consensus survey has been taken, divide the staff into six teams of equal numbers and process the group responses for each consensus survey question by responding to the following three prompts: (1) What are the facts? (2) What implications or conclusions can we draw from the survey? (3) What are our next steps for improvement?

Here's What! (What are the facts?)	**So What?** (What implications and conclusions can we draw?)	**Now What?** (What are our next steps for improvement?)
1.		
2.		
3.		
4.		
5.		
6.		

Figure 6.15: School culture survey.

Visit ***go.SolutionTree.com/instruction*** *for a free reproducible version of this figure.*

well-being. Our mindset matters. Creating a positive culture in which we work with others matters, whether in a classroom, a school building, or the whole district. The brain can regroup, evolve, and grow due to its neuroplasticity. New nerve cells are being birthed every day with our thoughts, and it is our choice whether our experiences are positive or negative ones.

Our collective desire for all educators is not only to create a place where students think well but also to construct positive, healthy environments where humans *thrive*, not merely survive. As partners in creating a future of strong principles of learning, caring, and innovating, we join all of our dear colleagues in the challenge.

The Takeaways

To manage and lead the learning, consider the following points.

Managing teachers:

- Have a growth mindset about learning and students, and teach and promote a growth mindset in their students
- Build healthy learning environments that appropriately deal with off-task and disruptive behaviors, and build routines for smooth daily operations
- Use a wide variety of strategies to maintain order and a strong learning environment

Leading teachers:

- Think and build lessons from the inside out, beginning with the why of learning
- Are present in all professional settings
- Conduct and work toward skillful discussion, balancing advocacy and inquiry

Leading administrators:

- Build a collaborative community of professionals
- Lead staff from the inside out, beginning with the why of policy and procedure
- Use a variety of strategies and skillful conversations to build high-functioning teams

We began this manuscript by stating, "In some ways, this entire book is about planning—thoughtful, systematic planning with the end in mind." We have purposefully planned each chapter in order to create a detailed big picture of what that might look like in your classroom and at your campus, whether rural, urban, or suburban.

And we end this manuscript with all the confidence that *you*, our treasured colleagues, will continue to make a difference on behalf of our next generation.

APPENDIX

Putting the Pieces Together

The scope of this book has covered a broad range of topics with multiple details and examples. The following big-picture planning charts and visuals pull all the components together and support teachers in visualizing the big picture. We hope you find these figures helpful as you move forward in crafting Unstoppable Learning for our students.

Use figure A.1 to evaluate your current status on each of the Unstoppable Learning components: planning, launching, consolidating, assessing, adapting, managing, and leading. This tool can be used individually or as a team.

Unstoppable Practices	Actions	Current Reality	Specific Next Steps
Planning Learning	Establish priority standards.	1 2 3 4 5	
	Create scope and sequence in the unit planner (figure 1.1, pages 8–9).	1 2 3 4 5	
	Determine DOK (table 3.1, page 38).	1 2 3 4 5	
Launching Learning	Develop student *I can* statements.	1 2 3 4 5	
	Plan prime-time 1 and prime-time 2 activities (pages 26–27).	1 2 3 4 5	
	Plan the launch (figure 2.6, page 31).	1 2 3 4 5	
Consolidating Learning	Try new instructional strategies:		
	Relationship tasks	1 2 3 4 5	
	Window pane	1 2 3 4 5	
	Top hat organizer	1 2 3 4 5	
	Think Dots	1 2 3 4 5	
	Role, audience, format, and topic (RAFT) activity	1 2 3 4 5	
	Graphic organizers	1 2 3 4 5	
	Socratic seminar	1 2 3 4 5	
	Peer or rally coaching	1 2 3 4 5	
	Elevator speech	1 2 3 4 5	
	Other:	1 2 3 4 5	

Figure A.1: Unstoppable Learning planning template.

continued →

Unstoppable Practices	Actions	Current Reality	Specific Next Steps
Assessing Learning	Plan preassessments (figure 4.1, page 65).	1 2 3 4 5	
	Construct formative checks for understanding (figure 4.2, page 67).	1 2 3 4 5	
	Design summative assessments (page 68).	1 2 3 4 5	
	Construct a learning target chart to track growth.	1 2 3 4 5	
	Interpret data (table 4.5, page 81).	1 2 3 4 5	
	Engage students in self-reflection.	1 2 3 4 5	
Adapting Learning	Administer student surveys (figures 5.5 and 5.6, page 100).	1 2 3 4 5	
	Give assignment options (figure 5.4, page 97).	1 2 3 4 5	
	Differentiate according to content, process, product, or student learning preference (table 5.1, page 103).	1 2 3 4 5	
Managing and Leading Learning	Use management strategies reflection sheet (figure 6.2, page 111).	1 2 3 4 5	
	Complete the compass activity (figure 6.13, page 126).	1 2 3 4 5	
	Examine and discuss inquiry and advocacy conversations (figure 6.9, page 120).	1 2 3 4 5	
	Create SMART goals (figure 6.12, page 125).	1 2 3 4 5	
	Process by using the What, So What, Now What? template (figure 6.14, page 127).	1 2 3 4 5	
	Engage in the six domains of highly effective schools activity (figure 6.11, page 124).	1 2 3 4 5	
	Complete personal reflections on the following statements:		
	I have a positive mindset.	1 2 3 4 5	
	I have a renewed commitment to our vision.	1 2 3 4 5	
	I lead by example.	1 2 3 4 5	
	I have provided multiple opportunities to work in collaboration with others to encourage a systems approach.	1 2 3 4 5	

Current Reality

1 = awareness but no use

2 = beginning to use

3 = routine practice

4 = routine practice and beginning refinement

5 = established use and ongoing refinement

Visit ***go.SolutionTree.com/instruction*** *for a free reproducible version of this figure.*

While we have offered strategies and considerations throughout this book and especially in chapter 6 for building collaborative teams and schoolwide or districtwide systems that are enriching and effective, this does not happen immediately. Rather, it happens over time. The development of effective systems usually happens in five phases, as shown in figure A.2.

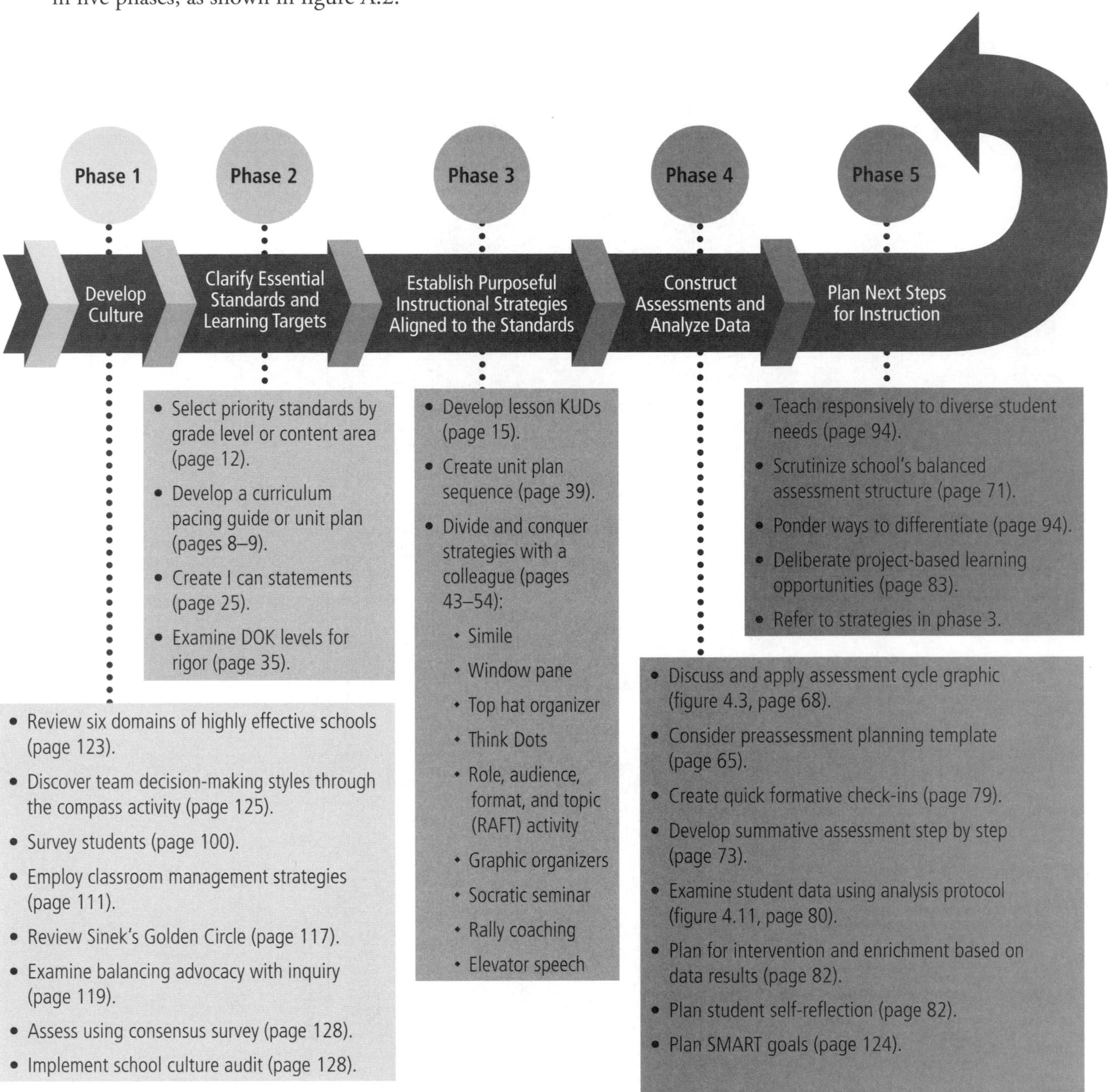

Phase 1
Phase 2
Phase 3
Phase 4
Phase 5
Develop Culture
Clarify Essential Standards and Learning Targets
Establish Purposeful Instructional Strategies Aligned to the Standards
Construct Assessments and Analyze Data
Plan Next Steps for Instruction
• Review six domains of highly effective schools (page 123).
• Discover team decision-making styles through the compass activity (page 125).
• Survey students (page 100).
• Employ classroom management strategies (page 111).
• Review Sinek's Golden Circle (page 117).
• Examine balancing advocacy with inquiry (page 119).
• Assess using consensus survey (page 128).
• Implement school culture audit (page 128).
• Select priority standards by grade level or content area (page 12).
• Develop a curriculum pacing guide or unit plan (pages 8–9).
• Create I can statements (page 25).
• Examine DOK levels for rigor (page 35).
• Develop lesson KUDs (page 15).
• Create unit plan sequence (page 39).
• Divide and conquer strategies with a colleague (pages 43–54):
• Simile
• Window pane
• Top hat organizer
• Think Dots
• Role, audience, format, and topic (RAFT) activity
• Graphic organizers
• Socratic seminar
• Rally coaching
• Elevator speech
• Discuss and apply assessment cycle graphic (figure 4.3, page 68).
• Consider preassessment planning template (page 65).
• Create quick formative check-ins (page 79).
• Develop summative assessment step by step (page 73).
• Examine student data using analysis protocol (figure 4.11, page 80).
• Plan for intervention and enrichment based on data results (page 82).
• Plan student self-reflection (page 82).
• Plan SMART goals (page 124).
• Teach responsively to diverse student needs (page 94).
• Scrutinize school's balanced assessment structure (page 71).
• Ponder ways to differentiate (page 94).
• Deliberate project-based learning opportunities (page 83).
• Refer to strategies in phase 3.

Figure A.2 Developmental phases of Unstoppable Learning for collaborative teams.

*Visit **go.SolutionTree.com/instruction** for a free reproducible version of this figure.*

Lastly, figure A.3 (page 134) provides an illustration for another way to help teachers see how curriculum, instruction, and assessment all work together.

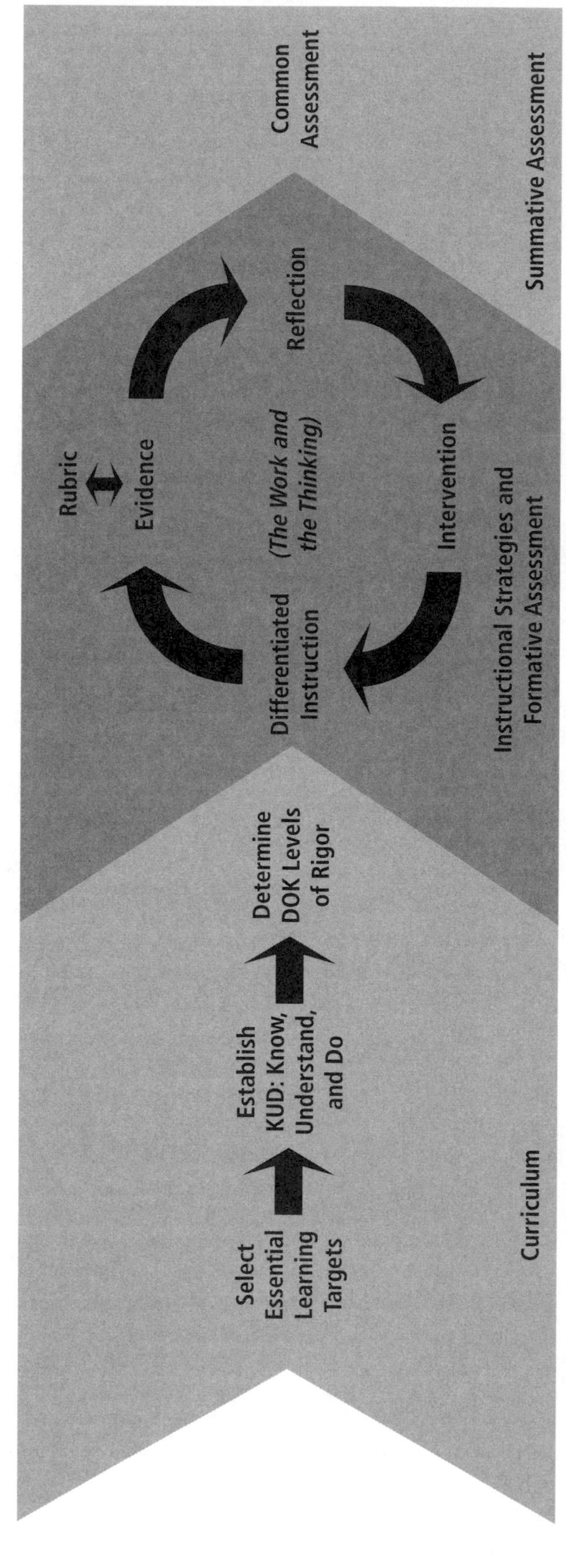

Figure A.3: Establishing the CIA—curriculum, instruction, assessment.

References and Resources

Ainsworth, L. (2010). *Rigorous curriculum design: How to create curricular units of study that align standards, instruction, and assessment.* Englewood, CO: Lead and Learn Press.

Allen, M., Noel, R. C., Rienzi, B. M., & McMillin, D. J. (2002). *Outcomes assessment handbook*. Long Beach: California State University, Institute for Teaching and Learning.

Anderson, L. W., & Krathwohl, D. (Eds.). (2001). *A taxonomy for learning, teaching, and assessing: A revision of Bloom's taxonomy of educational objectives*. Boston: Allyn & Bacon.

Au, K., & Mason, J. (1981). Social organizational factors in learning to read: The balance of rights hypothesis. *Reading Research Quarterly*, *17*(1), 115–152.

Bill and Melinda Gates Foundation. (n.d.). *Continued progress: Promising evidence on personalized learning*. Accessed at http://k12education.gatesfoundation.org/wp-content/uploads/2015/11/Personalized-Learning-RAND-Fact-Sheet.pdf on January 25, 2017.

Billmeyer, R., & Barton, M. L. (2002). *Teaching reading in the content areas: If not me, then who?* (2nd ed.). Aurora, CO: McREL.

Black, P., & Wiliam, D. (1998). *Inside the black box: Raising standards through classroom assessment* [Booklet]. London: King's College.

Blood, E., & Neel, R. (2008). Using student response systems in lecture-based instruction: Does it change student engagement and learning? *Journal of Technology and Teacher Education*, *16*(3), 375–383.

Bloom, B. S. (Ed.). (1956). *Taxonomy of educational objectives: Book 1—Cognitive domain*. New York: Longman.

Bosworth, P. (2016). *Coaching vs. directing: How to be a leader people want to follow*. Accessed at http://insights.leadershipchoice.com/coaching-vs.-directing-how-to-be-a-leader-people-want-to-follow on January 23, 2017.

Brophy, J. (2008). Developing students' appreciation for what is taught in school. *Educational Psychologist*, *43*(3), 132–141.

Collins, J. (2001). *Good to great: Why some companies make the leap—And others don't.* New York: HarperBusiness.

Conzemius, A. E., & O'Neill, J. (2014). *The handbook for SMART school teams: Revitalizing best practices for collaboration* (2nd ed.). Bloomington, IN: Solution Tree Press.

Cornelius-White, J. (2007). Learner-centered teacher-student relationships are effective: A meta-analysis. *Review of Educational Research*, *77*(1), 113–143.

Coyle, D. (2009). *The talent code: Unlocking the secret of skill in sports, art, music, math, and just about anything.* Minneapolis, MN: HighBridge.

Critical and Analytical Thinking Skills. (n.d.). Accessed at https://he.palgrave.com/studentstudyskills/page/critical-and-analytical-thinking-skills/ on January 24, 2017.

Diamond, M., & Hopson, J. (1999). *Magic trees of the mind: How to nurture your child's intelligence, creativity, and healthy emotions from birth through adolescence.* New York: Plume.

DuFour, R., DuFour, R., Eaker, R., Many, T., & Mattos, M. (2016). *Learning by doing: A handbook for Professional Learning Communities at Work* (3rd ed.). Bloomington, IN: Solution Tree Press.

Dweck, C. (2006). *Mindset: The new psychology of success.* New York: Random House.

Eggen, P., & Kauchak, D. (2001). *Educational psychology: Windows on classrooms* (5th ed.). Upper Saddle River, NJ: Prentice Hall.

Ferriter, B. (2012). *How guaranteed and viable is your curriculum?* Accessed at www.teachingquality.org/content/blogs/bill-ferriter/how-guaranteed-and-viable-your-curriculum-handouts on January 18, 2017.

Ferriter, B. (2015, November). *Singletons in a PLC.* Presentation at Reaching New Heights: PLC at Work Associate Retreat, Salt Lake City, UT.

Fisher, D. (2015, March). Presentation at Solution Tree Unstoppable Learning training, San Diego, CA.

Fisher, D., & Frey, N. (2015). *Unstoppable learning: Seven essential elements to unleash student potential.* Bloomington, IN: Solution Tree Press.

Frey, N., & Fisher, D. (2011). *The formative assessment action plan: Practical steps to more successful teaching and learning.* Alexandria, VA: Association for Supervision and Curriculum Development.

Gallagher, K. (2009). *Readicide: How schools are killing reading and what you can do about it.* Portland, ME: Stenhouse.

Gardner, H. (1983). *Frames of mind: The theory of multiple intelligences.* New York: Basic Books.

Global Digital Citizen Foundation. (n.d.). *Project based learning in the classroom: Solution fluency project ideas, year 6–9.* Accessed at http://cdn2.hubspot.net/hubfs/452492/content/PBL_69.pdf?t=1456642369526 on September 14, 2016.

Green, E. (2014, July 23). Why do Americans stink at math? *New York Times Magazine.* Accessed at www.nytimes.com/2014/07/27/magazine/why-do-americans-stink-at-math.html?emc=eta1&_r=0 on June 22, 2016.

Hattie, J. (2012). *Visible learning for teachers: Maximizing impact on learning.* London: Routledge.

Hattie, J., Fisher, D., & Frey, N. (2017). *Visible learning for mathematics, grades K–12: What works best to optimize student learning.* Thousand Oaks, CA: Corwin Press.

Heacox, D. (2012). *Differentiating instruction in the regular classroom: How to reach and teach all learners.* Minneapolis, MN: Free Spirit.

Hess, K. (2003). *Depth of knowledge (DOK) levels for writing.* Dover, NH: Center for Assessment. Accessed at http://storage.cloversites.com/teachforamericacolorado/documents/DOK%20Writing.pdf on January 25, 2017.

Kanold, T. D. (2011). *The five disciplines of PLC leaders.* Bloomington, IN: Solution Tree Press.

Kanold, T. D., & Larson, M. R. (2012). *Common Core mathematics in a PLC at Work, leader's guide.* Bloomington, IN: Solution Tree Press.

Kelly, M. (2004). *The rhythm of life: Living every day with passion and purpose.* New York: Fireside.

Lapp, D., Moss, B., Grant, M. C., & Johnson, K. (2016). *Turning the page on complex texts: Differentiated scaffolds for close reading instruction.* Bloomington, IN: Solution Tree Press.

Leskes, A. (2002). Beyond confusion: An assessment glossary. *Peer Review, 4*(2/3). Accessed at www.aacu.org/publications-research/periodicals/beyond-confusion-assessment-glossary on March 7, 2017.

Lindsay Unified School District. (n.d.). *Lindsay Unified School District: Mission statement.* Accessed at www.lindsay.k12.ca.us/filelibrary/LUSD%20Strategic%20Design%201.pdf on March 6, 2017.

Lindsay Unified School District. (2017). *Beyond reform: Systemic shifts toward personalized learning.* Bloomington, IN: Marzano Research.

Marzano, R. J. (2003). *What works in schools: Translating research into action.* Alexandria, VA: Association for Supervision and Curriculum Development.

Marzano, R. J. (2007). *The art and science of teaching: A comprehensive framework for effective instruction.* Alexandria, VA: Association for Supervision and Curriculum Development.

Mayo Clinic. (2017). *Mayo Clinic mission and values.* Accessed at www.mayoclinic.org/about-mayo-clinic/mission-values on January 18, 2017.

McTighe, J., & Wiggins, G. (2013). *Essential questions: Opening doors to student understanding.* Alexandria, VA: Association for Supervision and Curriculum Development.

Mississippi Department of Education. (2009). *Webb's Depth of Knowledge guide: Career and technical education definitions*. Accessed at www.aps.edu/rande/documents/resources/Webbs_DOK_Guide.pdf on June 22, 2016.

National Governors Association Center for Best Practices & Council of Chief State School Officers. (2010a). *Common Core State Standards for English language arts and literacy in history/social studies, science, and technical subjects*. Washington, DC: Authors. Accessed at www.corestandards.org/assets/CCSSI_ELA%20Standards.pdf on November 21, 2016.

National Governors Association Center for Best Practices & Council of Chief State School Officers. (2010b). *Common Core State Standards for mathematics*. Washington, DC: Authors. Accessed at www.corestandards.org/assets/CCSSI_Math%20Standards.pdf on November 21, 2016.

New York City Department of Education. (n.d.). *New York City Department of Education: 9–12 social studies scope and sequence 2014–2015*. New York: Author. Accessed at http://schools.nyc.gov/NR/rdonlyres/A739A67E-6228-4084-99C8-F890617D265B/0/scopeandsequence912_v6_web.pdf on March 6, 2017.

NGSS Lead States. (2013). *Next Generation Science Standards: For states, by states*. Washington, DC: National Academies Press.

Organisation for Economic Co-operation and Development. (n.d.). *PISA 2012 results*. Accessed at www.oecd.org/pisa/keyfindings/pisa-2012-results.htm on November 21, 2016.

Organisation for Economic Co-operation and Development. (2016). *PISA 2015 results in focus*. Accessed at www.oecd.org/pisa/pisa-2015-results-in-focus.pdf on January 24, 2017.

Palomba, C. A., & Banta, T. W. (1999). *Assessment essentials: Planning, implementing, and improving assessment in higher education*. San Francisco: Jossey-Bass.

Popham, W. J. (2008). *Transformative assessment*. Alexandria, VA: Association for Supervision and Curriculum Development.

Popham, W. J. (2011). *Transformative assessment in action: An inside look at applying the process*. Alexandria, VA: Association for Supervision and Curriculum Development.

Potter, A., Whitener, A., & Sikorsky, J. (2016, February 29). *Curriculum of the 21st century* [Blog post]. Accessed at www.envisionexperience.com/blog/curriculum-of-the-21st-century on January 24, 2017.

Reeves, D. (2016). *FAST grading: A guide to implementing best practices*. Bloomington, IN: Solution Tree Press.

Richardson, D. (2013). *21st century skills*. Accessed at https://prezi.com/tusqr0f4vmwp/21st-century-skills/ on January 24, 2017.

Scherer, M. (2001). How and why standards can improve student achievement: A conversation with Robert J. Marzano. *Educational Leadership*, *59*(1), 14–18.

Schlechty, P. C. (2011). *Engaging students: The next level of working on the work*. San Francisco: Jossey-Bass.

Schmidt, W., Houang, R., & Cogan, L. (2002). A coherent curriculum: The case of mathematics. *American Educator*, *26*(2), 10–26, 47.

Schmoker, M. (2011). *Focus: Elevating the essentials to radically improve student learning*. Alexandria, VA: Association for Supervision and Curriculum Development.

School Reform Initiative. (2007). *Compass points: North, south, east, and west—An exercise in understanding preferences in group work*. Accessed at http://schoolreforminitiative.org/doc/compass_points.pdf on January 23, 2017.

Senge, P. (2006). *The fifth discipline: The art and practice of the learning organization* (Rev. and updated ed.). New York: Doubleday.

Senge, P., Kleiner, A., Roberts, C., Ross, R., & Smith, B. (1994). *The fifth discipline fieldbook: Strategies and tools for building a learning organization*. New York: Currency.

Silver, H. F., Dewing, R. T., & Perini, M. J. (2012). *The core six: Essential strategies for achieving excellence with the Common Core*. Alexandria, VA: Association for Supervision and Curriculum Development.

Sinek, S. (2009a, September). *Simon Sinek: How great leaders inspire action* [Video file]. Accessed at www.ted.com/talks/simon_sinek_how_great_leaders_inspire_action?language=en on June 22, 2016.

Sinek, S. (2009b). *Start with why: How great leaders inspire everyone to take action*. New York: Portfolio.

Sinek, S. (2014). *Leaders eat last: Why some teams pull together and others don't*. New York: Portfolio.

Sizer, T. R. (2004). *Horace's compromise: The dilemma of the American high school.* Boston: Houghton Mifflin.

Smith, M. S., & Stein, M. K. (2011). *5 practices for orchestrating productive mathematics discussions.* Reston, VA: National Council of Teachers of Mathematics.

Smith, N. N. (2017). *A mind for mathematics: Meaningful teaching and learning in elementary classrooms.* Bloomington, IN: Solution Tree Press.

Sousa, D. A. (2015). *How the brain learns mathematics* (2nd ed.). Thousand Oaks, CA: Corwin Press.

Sternberg, R. J. (2005). The theory of successful intelligence. *Interamerican Journal of Psychology, 39*(2), 189–202.

Stiggins, R., & Chappuis, J. (2006). What a difference a word makes: Assessment FOR learning rather than assessment OF learning helps students succeed. *Journal of Staff Development, 27*(1), 10–14.

Tomlinson, C. A. (2001). *How to differentiate instruction in mixed-ability classrooms* (2nd ed.). Alexandria, VA: Association for Supervision and Curriculum Development.

Tomlinson, C. A. (2014). *The differentiated classroom: Responding to the needs of all learners* (2nd ed.). Alexandria, VA: Association for Supervision and Curriculum Development.

Tomlinson, C. A., Brimijoin, K., & Narvaez, L. (2008). *The differentiated school: Making revolutionary changes in teaching and learning.* Alexandria, VA: Association for Supervision and Curriculum Development.

Turville, J. (2007). *Differentiating by student interest: Practical lessons and strategies.* Larchmont, NY: Eye on Education.

Vagle, N. D. (2015). *Design in five: Essential phases to create engaging assessment practice.* Bloomington, IN: Solution Tree Press.

Vagle, N. D. (2016). *Keeping assessment balanced: The standardized test effect.* Accessed at http://allthingsassessment.info/2016/09/01/keeping-assessment-balanced-the-standardized-test-effect on February 1, 2017.

Valdellon, L. (2015, May 13). *Why every company needs a culture of collaboration* [Blog post]. Accessed at www.wrike.com/blog/every-company-needs-culture-collaboration-slideshare on June 22, 2016.

van Munster, B., & Weinstein, E. (Directors). (2001). *The amazing race* [Television series]. Los Angeles: CBS Television Studios.

Walton, D. (2012). *Emotional intelligence: A practical guide.* London: Icon Books.

West Virginia. (2016, December 22). *Tiny homes ceremony* [Video file]. Accessed at www.youtube.com/watch?v=8nLO8p4g_Hc&feature=youtu.be on January 20, 2017.

West Virginia Department of Education. (n.d.). *West Virginia Simulated Workplace operational manual.* Accessed at https://wvde.state.wv.us/simulated-workplace/files/2015-simulated-workplace-manual.pdf on January 20, 2017.

Wiggins, G., & McTighe, J. (2011). *The understanding by design guide to creating high-quality units.* Alexandria, VA: Association for Supervision and Curriculum Development.

Wikipedia. (n.d.). *Programme for International Student Assessment.* Accessed at http://en.wikipedia.org/wiki/Programme_for_International_Student_Assessment on June 22, 2016.

Wiliam, D. (2011). *Embedded formative assessment.* Bloomington, IN: Solution Tree Press.

Wisconsin Center for Education Products and Services. (2014, July 1). *Dr. Norman Webb's DOK overview* [Video file]. Accessed at www.youtube.com/watch?v=qFXU6_TYIjc on June 22, 2016.

Wolfe, P. (2010). *Brain matters: Translating research into classroom practice* (2nd ed.). Alexandria, VA: Association for Supervision and Curriculum Development.

Wong, H. K., Wong, R. T., Jondahl, S. F., & Ferguson, O. F. (2014). *The classroom management book.* Mountain View, CA: Wong.

Index

L

M

N

O

P

Q

R

S

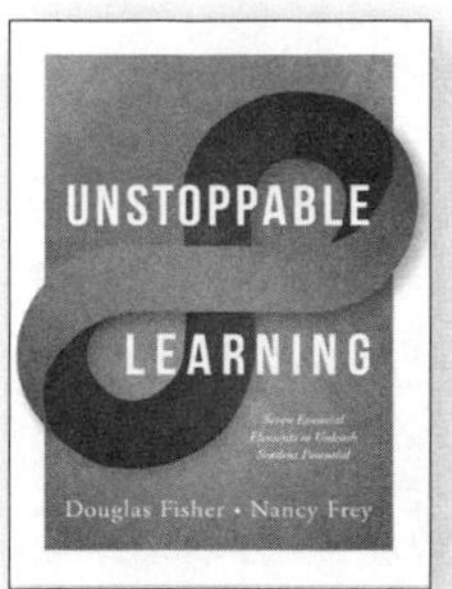

Unstoppable Learning
Douglas Fisher and Nancy Frey
Discover proven methods to enhance teaching and learning schoolwide. Identify questions educators should ask to guarantee a positive classroom culture where students learn from each other, not just teachers. Explore ways to adapt teaching in response to students' individual needs.
BKF662

A Mind for Mathematics
Nanci N. Smith
This easy-to-read text breaks down the complex components of mathematics teaching and divides them into practical strategies. Combining research, useful tactics, and examples from K–6 classrooms, the book includes reflection questions, action tasks, and activities to inspire and engage mathematical minds.
BKF724

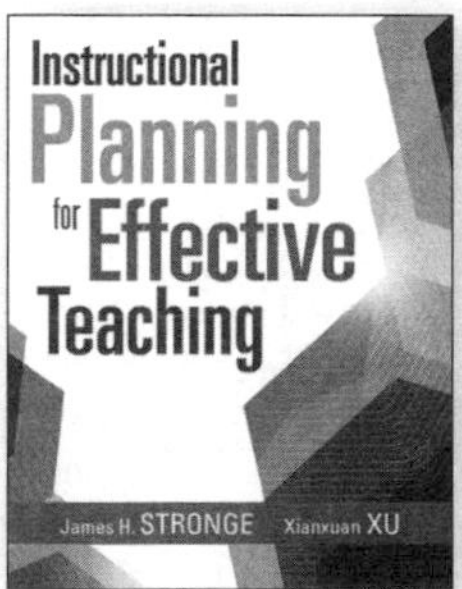

Instructional Planning for Effective Teaching
James H. Stronge and Xianxuan Xu
Explore research-based instructional planning tools teachers, leaders, and administrators can use in everyday practice. Discover powerful strategies and guidelines for developing quality lessons, setting learning objectives, planning differentiated instruction, and designing technology-integrated learning to effectively teach and challenge every student.
BKF642

Instructional Strategies for Effective Teaching
James H. Stronge and Xianxuan Xu
Discover research-based instructional strategies teachers, coaches, and administrators can use to enhance their everyday practices. Organized around ten methods of instruction, this user-friendly guide will help you dig deep into classroom discussion, concept mapping, inquiry-based learning, and more.
BKF641

The New Art and Science of Teaching
Robert J. Marzano
This title is a greatly expanded volume of the original *The Art and Science of Teaching*, offering a framework for substantive change based on Robert J. Marzano's fifty years of education research. While the previous model focused on teacher outcomes, the new version places focus on student outcomes.
BKF776